student

thinking like a christian

D0507310

david noebel
chuck edwards

Anecdotal illustrations used in this book are composites of real situations and any resemblance to people living or dead is coincidental.

Copyright ©1999 by Summit Press
Summit Ministries, P.O. Box 207, Manitou Springs, Colorado 80829
(719) 685-9103, www.summit.org

ISBN 0-936163-08-9

Unless indicated otherwise, Scripture quotations are from the Holy Bible, *New International Version,* ©1973, 1978, 1984 by the International Bible Society.

Printed in the United States of America.

mapping out the journey

straight talk from
best-selling author and speaker
josh mcdowell

Your generation is faced with the greatest and most rapid cultural changes in history. This cultural crisis is a result of a change in the way people view what is true.

I've given more than 23,000 talks to students in 1,000 universities and 2,000 high schools in 100 countries around the world. What I'm finding is this: when I make a statement about the deity of Christ, the resurrection, or the reliability of the scriptures, I have people come up to me and say, **"What right do you have to say that? You're being intolerant! What right do you have to judge anyone's moral life?"** These questions come from a totally different view of life. You probably realize that we no longer live in a Judeo-Christian culture based on principles from the Bible. Instead, we are now living in an anti-Christian culture!

That's why you face a challenge unlike any other in recent history.

And that brings me to the importance of this **student journal**. Before you can know how to respond to our changing culture, you must first understand how the Bible relates to all of life. In the pages of this **journal**, you will encounter a biblical worldview. Each daily session will be an eye-opening experience that gives hope, meaning and a greater understanding of how God fits into every part of your life.

My son was one of those who came face to face with a biblical worldview a few years ago when he attended a Summit Ministries conference. It was by far one of the most significant conferences he has ever attended. The impact will affect Sean the rest of his life. My seventeen year old daughter Katie went through the biblical worldview curriculum in her high school. This has prepared her for college; not only to survive, but to also thrive in her walk with Christ.

This **student journal** is based on the same information that Sean and Katie received. I challenge you to spend time in this **journal** each day. Then, like the leaders from the small tribe of Issachar in the Old Testament, you will **understand the times** and **know what you should do** (1 Chronicles 12:32).

josh

a journey of discovery

You are about to begin a journey into another world but not the kind of world you might imagine. These pages will take you on a journey into the world of the mind – the world of "ideas."

On this journey of discovery you will be challenged to compare your ideas about life with the ideas that come from the Bible. In the process, you will be forming a **"biblical worldview."**

Along the way you will meet two other fellow travelers. One is **Skip**. Known as "the skeptic," he is always questioning the Bible and challenging the faith of Christians. You may find that Skip raises some questions that you have struggled with from time to time. Be on the lookout for Skip. He tends to show up when you least expect him.

Then there is **Chris**. He's a rock-solid kind of guy. You'll find that Chris thinks through the important issues of life from a biblical point of view. What he has to say just might make sense to you, too.

"I don't believe in God"

Skip

where this journey is taking you

As you make this **journal** a part of your daily routine, you will begin to see the **big picture** of how the Bible relates to every area of life. The eleven weeks are divided into the following topics:

Chris

"O.K., who do you believe in?"

week	topic
1.	**introduction:** How the Bible relates to **every area of your life!**
2.	**theology:** What is God like, and what difference does it make?
3.	**philosophy:** What is reality, and how do we know what's true?
4.	**biology:** How did life originate, and what difference does it make?
5.	**psychology:** What is the basic nature of humanity?
6.	**ethics:** What makes some things right and other things wrong?
7.	**sociology:** What is the basis for a healthy society?
8.	**law:** Are there certain principles that rule our world and our lives?
9.	**politics:** How should government be organized?
10.	**economics:** What is the basis for making and spending money?
11.	**history:** What is the flow of history, and where is it going?

about this journal

This **journal** is designed to assist you in developing a worldview based on the Bible. Plan a time that you can spend each day, five days a week, to work on each session. You'll be amazed at how quickly you gain a whole new understanding of yourself, your relationship with God, and the world in which you live.

Some of the suggestions in this **journal** are designed for discussion during a weekly group study. If you are not involved in a group study on worldviews you can still complete these exercises. They will help you dig deeper into the world of ideas.

The major topics in this **journal** are taken from the book, *Understanding the Times* (Abridged Edition), by David A. Noebel. When this resource is quoted it will be set apart in a text box followed by (UTT, __) to indicate the page from which the quote is taken.

So hang in there; you're about to embark on a mind-expanding journey into the
➤ **world of ideas!**

Yours for the journey,
David Noebel and Chuck Edwards

removing the mental blinders

the "blinders phenomenon"

Blinders–you know, like a mule or a horse wearing blinders. The poor animal can only see what is directly in front of him. He knows nothing about the rest of the world except what is at his feet.

Christians can experience what's called the "blinders phenomenon." One Christian writer described it this way:

> **The basic problem of the Christians in this country [referring to America!] . . . is that they have seen things in bits and pieces instead of totals (UTT, 4).**

Seeing just "bits and pieces". . . it's like going through life wearing mental blinders. We can only see what's directly in front of us–not seeing the total picture.

To determine if you suffer from the "blinders phenomenon," take the following "test." Place a checkmark in front of each of the following statements that are true about you:

- ☐ I sometimes wonder if there is any purpose to my life.
- ☐ I have questions about whether the Bible is true.
- ☐ I'm not sure if Christianity is the only true religion.
- ☐ I believe that religious ideas and civil government should be kept separate.
- ☐ All religions ultimately lead to God.

wow!

Our problem is not seeing the big picture.

☐ I think people are basically good; it's just that they are raised in bad circumstances which may lead them to commit a crime.

☐ Religious talk of a "Creator" should not be used in a public school science class.

☐ Christianity is my religion, but it may not be right for other people.

☐ The world would be a happier place if the wealthy were taxed more and the money was given to those less fortunate.

☐ When it comes to morality, what's right for you might not be right for me.

Count the check marks and write the total number here: _____

a personal "eye" exam

How well do you "see" the world from a biblical perspective? If you checked **less than three statements**, then you are experiencing only a slight "blinder" problem. This means that you see things from a predominantly Christian perspective, but there are a few areas where you need to sharpen your vision. This journal will help you do that.

If you checked **4 to 6 statements**, your mental blinders have narrowed your vision. There are several areas that you do not understand from a biblical view point. Use this journal to help you to pry back the blinders to see the issues more clearly.

If you checked **more than 6 statements,** you have a severe case of the "blinders." However, it's not hopeless. By spending time each day in your journal and participating in a weekly group study, you will develop 20/20 vision for seeing the world of ideas through the lens of the Bible.

defining a worldview:

"A worldview is an overarching approach to understanding_____, (read the "check it out!" box to fill in the blanks.) the world, and _____ relations to God and the world" (UTT, 2). A worldview contains a particular perspective regarding each of the following ten categories: theology, philosophy, ethics, biology, psychology, sociology, law, politics, economics, and history. A worldview will also speak to other cultural issues, such as the arts.

What do you think? Does the Bible have something to say about each of these ten areas? (Check your answer)

☐ Yes!
☐ Maybe, convince me.
☐ Definitely not!

If you checked the second or third answer, then hang in there. Keep interacting with your journal and coming to the group sessions. Over the next several weeks, you will have an eye-opening experience as each of the ten categories will be discussed in light of principles found in the Bible!

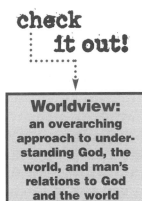

check it out!

Worldview: an overarching approach to understanding God, the world, and man's relations to God and the world (UTT, 2).

pray about it!

This week's key verses are Colossians 2:6-7. As you read them, think about how you should live in Christ.

---

week 1 key verses: **Colossians 2:6-7**

"So then, just as you received Christ Jesus as Lord, continue to live in him, rooted and built up in him, strengthened in the faith as you were taught, and overflowing with thankfulness."

Write a prayer asking God to remove any mental blinders that are keeping you from seeing the world through biblical eyes.

_____

_____

_____

_____

day 1 summary:

Many Christians fail to understand that the Bible presents a total worldview.

thinking like a christian
thinking about thinking

How would you rather spend an evening? (check one)

- [ ] reading a novel and discussing the plot and character development with a friend

- [ ] watching a high action movie with a romantic encounter between the leading male and female actors

Most people would rather be entertained than read a book! Let's face it, thinking is hard work! It's much easier to watch a movie or just listen to your favorite CD.

But the movies you watch and the music you listen to are filled with ideas about life. And whether you realize it or not, these ideas impact the way you think. It's important to understand these ideas that are shaping your life.

"Thinking gives

me a headache"

As you continue through this **journal** you will see that thinking has its own rewards, rewards which are more meaningful than a popular movie and longer lasting than the latest hit CD.

thinking like a christian

Being a Christian is more than just doing "religious" things like devotional Bible reading, praying and staying away from sinful habits. We should be able to *think* like a Christian, too.

In fact, the Bible has a lot to say about the importance of using your mind when it comes to being a Christian.

> **Love the Lord your God with all your heart and with all your soul and with all your mind. This is the first and greatest commandment (Matthew 22:37-38).**

Jesus said that! Not only are you to love God with your heart and soul, but you are also to love God with all your _____!

What does it mean to love God with your **mind?**

_____

_____

In addition to loving God with all your mind, there is another biblical principle we should follow. Paul wrote in Romans 12:2,

> **Do not conform any longer to the pattern of this world, but be transformed by the renewing of your mind. Then you will be able to test and approve what God's will is—his good, pleasing and perfect will.**

Here, Paul talks about knowing God's will for your life. He says that you come to know God's will by _____ ____ _____ .

your mind matters

Jesus said that our minds are involved in loving God, and Paul mentions that we must renew our minds in order to know God's will. In light of these two principles, how important is it to learn to think like a Christian in each worldview category? (Circle your answer)

Very Important	Somewhat Important	Unimportant

1   2   3   4   5   6   7   8   9   10

Your mind really does matter. Being a Christian is so much more than just a personal, private relationship with God. Christianity extends to every aspect of your life. It is a total **worldview**.

wow!
Loving God means **thinking** like a Christian.

Over the next eleven weeks, you will learn to think, really think. You will find out how the Bible relates to each of the ten major areas that make up a total worldview.

put on your thinking cap!

Let's think like Christians! Grab a newspaper and scan the front page headlines.

1) **Pick an article** that you find interesting. Now, think about the big idea of the article. Does it fit into one of the ten worldview categories? Which one? Write the category at the top of the article.

3) **Bring the article** with you to the next group meeting to share with the rest of the group. (Make sure they are sitting down–it may overwhelm them that you have actually read the newspaper and thought about it!)

See how much fun thinking can be? You may even want to try it again sometime. Well, maybe you better wait a few days. . .you don't want to overwork your brain the first day! (Just kidding!)

pray . . . then go!

But before you go, take a minute to thank God for the wonderful mind that He has given you. Ask Him to expand your understanding of the Bible's view of life, your life, and how you fit into His world.

day 2 summary:

Loving God means learning to think in Christian categories.

is it secular or is it sacred?
mind your own business

> Many people believe that when Christians. . . attempt to speak to such "worldly" disciplines as politics, economics, biology, and law, they are overstepping their bounds. "Mind your own business," we are told. . . . **In short, isn't there a difference between the secular and the sacred?** (UTT, 13)

As you started on this journey into the world of ideas, maybe you've been asking the same questions: **"Shouldn't we 'mind our own business?' " "Why waste my time on 'worldly' issues?"**

secular vs. sacred

Is there a difference between the secular and the sacred? What do you think?

☐ Yes, there is a difference between the secular and the sacred.

☐ No, there is no difference between the two; everything is secular.

☐ No, there is no difference between the two; everything is sacred.

☐ I'm not sure; convince me!

Give reasons for your answer:

_____

_____

_____

_____

_____

check it out!

Secular: those areas of life that relate to this world and not to religion.

Sacred: areas in life that relate only to religion and religious principles.

thinking about "reality"

To settle the question about the secular and the sacred, read the following quote from Dietrich Bonhoeffer, a respected German theologian:

> There are not two realities, but only one reality, and that is the reality of God, which has become manifest in Christ in the reality of the world (UTT, 13).

How many realities are there? _____
What is that one reality? _____

If God created the world as one reality, wouldn't it make sense that we should think about everything the way God does?

From the Biblical Christian perspective, the ten categories addressed in this study reflect various attributes of God and His creative order. God created mankind with theological, philosophical, ethical, biological, psychological, sociological, legal, political, economic and historical dimensions. We all live within these categories. Why? Because that's the way God created us.

God's creative order

In the following passages, look at each example of God's creation.
Use your Bible and the categories below to fill in the missing words:

theology   sociology
philosophy   law
biology   politics
psychology   economics
ethics   history

Genesis 1:1 "In the beginning God _____ the heavens and the earth" is
value-laden with _____ and philosophical ramifications.

Genesis 2:9 "knowledge of good and evil"———➤ contains _____ ramifications.

Genesis 1:21 "after their _____" ——➤ biology.

Genesis 2:7 "a living being" ——➤ _____.

Genesis 1:28 "be fruitful and increase in number; fill the earth" ——➤ _____
and ecology.

Genesis 3:11 "I _____ you" ——➤ law.

Genesis 9:6 "whoever sheds the blood of man" ——➤ politics and_____.

Genesis 1:29 "it shall be for food" ——➤ economics.

Genesis 3:15 "enmity between thee and the _____" ——➤ history.

All ten categories are addressed in just the first few chapters of the Bible because they
manifest and accent certain aspects of God's creative order. God designed the world
to work in this way.

now, what do you think?

So which is it, secular or sacred? Take a wild guess and fill in the following sentence:

After careful consideration of the Scriptures, I believe all of life is_____.

thinking and praying

1) **Think** about an area in your life that you are keeping in a 'secular' box.
What would that be?

_____

2) **Now consider** God's view on that issue.
(A good place to look for God's perspective is in the Bible)

_____

_____

3) **Pray** about your commitment to live according to God's worldview as you clarify
it in writing:

_____

_____

day 3 summary:

It is true that Christians should mind their own business, BUT. . . everything is a Christian's business!

Review key verses: **Colossians 2:6-7**

"So then, just as you received Christ Jesus as Lord, continue to live in him, _____ and _____ in him, strengthened in the faith as you were taught, and overflowing with thankfulness."

---

western civilization and the bible
athletic shoes and worldviews

Why do you wear Nikes®? (No, it's not because they're cool or they make you run faster and jump higher.)

The question is, why do you wear expensive sports shoes instead of walking around barefoot? (No, it's not about comfort.)

Why do you even have all the different options of shoes to wear, instead of bare shelves staring you in the face?

Don't have a clue? If not, maybe it's because you usually don't think about things in that way. When you think on this level, you're using a worldview perspective.

You see, people living in India or the jungles of South America do not wear expensive athletic shoes. Know why? It has to do with their understanding of life–their worldview. Read on to find out how.

western civilization 101

The culture of western Europe and North America is called "western civilization." Western civilization grew out of a biblical point of view. As a result of this biblical mind set, science flourished. This in turn led to modern technology, a free market economy, greater prosperity for more people, and, you guessed it, Nikes®!

But it all started with a certain way of looking at life, a worldview based not on Buddhism, not on Hinduism, not on paganism, not on Humanism, . . . but **on the Bible.**

But this does not mean that a biblical worldview only relates to people in Europe and North America. The point is that Biblical Christianity is true for everybody everywhere because it contains true statements about the real world in which we live.

the christian worldview relates to all of life

In fact, you can find the truth of Christianity wherever you look. For example, George Gilder is not only an outstanding economic philosopher but also a sociologist who became a Christian while seeking sociological truth.

> "Christianity is true," says George Gilder, "and it's truth will be discovered **anywhere** you look very far" (UTT, 3).

List some of the "anywhere's" that a person might look to discover the truth of Christianity:

_____

_____

_____

Did your list include any of the ten categories that make up a worldview? If not, should you add those categories to your list? (**hint:** "Yes" would be a good answer!)

the heart of a biblical worldview

The center of a biblical worldview is found in the following verses from **Colossians 2:6,8:**

> **So then, just as you received Christ Jesus as Lord, continue to live in him. . . . See to it that no one takes you captive through hollow and deceptive philosophy, which depends on human tradition and the basic principles of this world rather than on Christ.**

"Philosophy" is another word for "worldview." These verses say that you should beware of _____ and _____ philosophy.

What does Paul mean by a deceptive philosophy? _____

_____

_____

Can you think of any current examples where "human tradition" is contrary to a Christian worldview? _____

_____

_____

In what ways can you be captured by deceitful philosophies or human traditions?

_____

_____

_____

_____

A biblical worldview is founded on Jesus Christ. As you continue your journey into the world of ideas, you will be discovering how Jesus is the center of every aspect of life. . . your life and everything you do.

If you are wearing Nikes® today (or any other brand of athletic shoe), you can literally thank Jesus for it! Apart from Him, we might be going barefoot!

pray about it

Review the words to "My World View" by Audio Adrenalin (printed below) and ask God to allow you to see the world through Jesus' eyes.

day 4 summary:

Christianity is true everywhere you look.

my world view

BY: Audio Adrenaline
don't censor me, 1993

I want to see the world through Jesus' eyes, see through Jesus tears.
I want to see the world through Jesus' eyes, my vision's not as clear.
I want to feel the world with the hands that made it, know the pain and appreciate it,
Hear their cries and hope to understand.

chorus
My world view, it's how I see the world, it's how I look at you.
My world view, it's how I see the world, would you like to see it too?
My world view.

I want to place my foot upon the rock, the rock that doesn't move.
For upon the rock the Kingdom's built, and here's the Kingdom view.
I see creation and I see Adam's fall, I see through the years and I can see it all.
All things come together for the good.

chorus II
My world view, it's how I see the world, it's how I look at you.
My world view, it's how I see the world, would you like to see it too?
My world view, it's how I see the world, would you like to see it too?

chorus III
My world view, I can see, I can see it forever.
It's how I see the world, it's how I look at you.
My world view, coming into view, coming into full view, it's how I see the world,
would you like to see it too?

Coming into view, coming into view, coming into full view.

the foundation of a biblical worldview

why the "leaning tower" is leaning

What's the most important part of a building? _____

While there are many parts to a building - floors, walls, roof, windows, doors - any builder will tell you that the most important part is the foundation. If the foundation is not laid correctly, then the entire building could crumble.

Why is the "Leaning Tower" of Pisa leaning? Because it's foundation was not laid correctly. In a similar way, it is important to start with a solid foundation for building a worldview.

foundations are important

What would you say is the foundation for a Biblical Christian worldview?

_____

Some people would say that the Bible is the foundation. But the Bible is simply the way that God has chosen to communicate His truth to us. It is not the foundation itself.

Someone else might choose "faith" as the foundation. But faith is our response to God's truth. It is not the foundation, itself.

Jesus - a rock solid foundation for your worldview!

Others say that God is the foundation. This is getting closer, but **Colossians 1:15** makes it even more specific. Look up that verse and fill in the blanks:

> He (Jesus Christ) is the _____ of the invisible God, the _____ over all creation.

This verse tells us that Jesus is "God made visible to us." We can comprehend God by looking at Jesus. And Jesus is the "most important thing" over all the created universe.

Jesus, the solid rock

Look at the rest of that passage in **Colossians 1** to find other reasons that Jesus is the starting point of a biblical worldview:

> 17 He is before all things, and in him all things hold together.
> 18 And he is the head of the body, the church; he is the beginning

and the firstborn from among the dead, so that in everything he might have the supremacy. 19 For God was pleased to have all his fullness dwell in him, 20 and through him to reconcile to himself all things, whether things on earth or things in heaven, by making peace through his blood, shed on the cross.

Jesus . . . . . .

_____ everything together.

. . . is the _____ of the church.

. . . has _____ over everything else, including death.

. . . is the _____ of God.

. . . _____ everything to himself through his shed_____ .

Do you get the idea that Jesus is the most important thing in the entire universe? This passage indicates that Jesus is a **solid foundation** for developing a worldview based on the Bible.

Jesus is the foundation

> When Christ told the woman who spoke of the Messiah, "I who speak to you am he" (John 4:26), He was telling her the most fundamental truth of all. What Christ said concerning life and death, the saved and lost condition of mankind, body and soul, and truth constitutes the central precepts of the Christian worldview. Christ is its cornerstone. He is the way, the truth, and the life (John 14:6) (UTT, 20).

Taking Christ out of our culture causes our society to fall apart, too. Do you see any evidences that our society is falling apart? What are they?

_____

_____

_____

_____

"Without a biblical worldview, society falls apart."

but, does this mean . . .?
(Circle your answer to the following questions)

. . . you can't separate religious ideas from how we run our government?

Yes / No

. . . science begins with assuming a Creator, namely, Jesus Christ?

Yes / No

. . . there are absolute moral standards such as saving sexual intimacy for marriage and not lying to my parents and not shooting my English teacher?

Yes / No

. . . I should speak up in class and share the reasons that Jesus is the beginning point for all knowledge?

Yes / No

If you answered YES to all of the above questions, you are well on your way to understanding the times from a biblical point of view.

it's something to think about . . . and pray about

Review today's lesson and pick one or two ideas that intrigue you the most. Maybe an item of praise for how Jesus is the cornerstone of your worldview. . . or maybe a personal application about speaking up for the truth in class. You decide . . . and pray.

day 5 summary:

Jesus Christ is the foundation of the Biblical Christian worldview.

 **summary:**

Life is like a gigantic jig-saw puzzle. When we put all the pieces together, a clear picture comes into focus. God designed the picture so that everything in it relates to Him, down to the smallest piece of the puzzle. The total picture is painted for us in the Bible. Jesus Christ is the foundation of the picture. We call this picture a **Biblical Christian worldview.**

> **Review** key verses: **Colossians 2:6-7**
> "So then, just as you received Christ Jesus as Lord, continue to live in him, rooted and built up in him, _____ in the faith as you were _____, and overflowing with thankfulness."

if you are involved in a group study on worldviews be sure to bring an article from the newspaper and your Bible to the next group meeting!

 theology
a close encounter of the "God" kind

Making sense out of our world is a pretty big task. You may sometimes feel confused and a little overwhelmed in trying to understand why people act in certain ways and why things happen the way they do. Your worldview helps you to put all the pieces together.

Putting together a worldview is much like working a puzzle—you start by finding the pieces that fit around the edge. The boundary pieces of any worldview start with the question: "What about God?" When we ask that question, we are dealing with the subject of "Theology."

"**Theology**" is simply the study of the existence, nature, and attributes of God. ◄········ Or, to put it another way, theology answers the following key questions: **Is there a God? What is God like?**

This week you will take a deeper look into both questions. During the process, you will. . .

> . . . encounter what it's like to take an atheist to lunch

> . . . make the connection between watches, minds, morals and God

> . . . learn that God has a special message for you

> . . . discover how God has personalized His communication to you in the person of Jesus Christ

To start looking for those outside pieces of your worldview, read on!

 God's spokesman
taking an atheist to lunch

One day in class you are introduced to a new student. Being the good Samaritan that you are, you volunteer to show the new guy, Skip, to the cafeteria to eat with you.

As you are munching on your spaghetti with meatballs, Skip tells you that his mom sued the last school he had attended because the coach had a prayer before the football games. He shows you his membership card with the American Atheist Association. You swallow some spaghetti as you weakly mumble that you go to church. He then asks you a question that makes you choke on your meatball and leaves a string of spaghetti dangling from your mouth: "So, you're a Christian. Tell me, how do you know there is a god?" At that precise moment, the entire cafeteria grows strangely silent and every person in the room turns and looks at you!

"Can you prove to me God exists?"

now what do you do?

(This is multiple choice – pick one)

☐ Drop to your knees and pray for God to help you.

☐ Start gaging on your meatball, rush out of the cafeteria into the bathroom and hide in one of the stalls until the final bell rings.

☐ Slurp up the spaghetti noodle with confidence, stand on top of the table and give a 30-minute discourse to the entire school on the rational basis of St. Aquines's five arguments for the existence of God.

☐ Whip out your cell phone, dial up your pastor and hand the phone over to Skip.

While you might not actually do any of the above, it's still a scary thing to think about the best way to answer the question Skip was asking: **"How do you know that God is real?"**

check it out!

General Revelation is God's communication of Himself to all persons, at all times, and in all places.

ask the heavens?

God has not left us alone to figure out what life is all about. Do you know how God has communicated to people everywhere, even those who cannot read? Can you name the terms Christians use to describe how God communicates to us through nature?

G_____ R_____ is God's communication of Himself to all persons, at all times, and in all places. This revelation from God allows all _____ everywhere, at any _____, and in every _____ to understand that **God is! He exists! He is real!**

the real communications network

In your Bible turn to Psalm 19. Read verses 1-4 as you answer the following questions:

1. Verse 1: What role does the physical universe play?

2. Verse 2: What two things does nature pour forth and display?

3. Verses 3 - 4: Is this knowledge of God communicated to people everywhere? Yes / No

4. In what way is it communicated?

Every person on planet Earth can hear and understand what nature is saying. In a big, loud voice it screams out **"God Is!"**

thinking like a christian

speaking out for God!

Because nature speaks so plainly, the Apostle Paul **spoke out** by writing that there is no excuse for anyone who does not believe in God.   Look up **Romans 1:20** and fill in the missing words (this text is from the NIV):

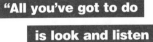

> For since the _____ of the world God's invisible qualities-- his eternal _____ and divine _____ -- have been clearly seen, being _____ from what has been made, so that men are without excuse.

This is why everywhere you go on our planet, you find cultures that believe in a Supreme Being. Nature has told them that God exists. From Paul's words, what two qualities does nature tell us about God?

1) E_____ P_____
2) D_____ N_____

In what ways does the universe display God's "eternal power?"

_____

_____

In what ways does the world show forth God's "divine nature?"

_____

_____

Paul concludes that no one anywhere at any time has an excuse for not knowing that GOD IS!

you are God's spokesperson!

Think of someone you know who may not be listening to God's communication through the natural world. Ask God to use you as His "Spokesperson" to that individual. Write the name of the person you are praying for: _____

day 1 summary:

All of creation declares that God is real.

---

week 2 key verse: **Colossians 2:9**

"For in Christ all the fullness of the Deity lives in bodily form. . . "

thinking like a christian

watches, minds and morals

a revealing riddle

Here's a riddle:

> What do watches, minds and morals have in common?
> (Take a minute to think about your answer and write it below:)

_____

_____

Time's up or "give up?"

The answer to the riddle is that each of the three things can be used to point to the reality of a "Supreme Being." Did you get it right? You might want to try that question on your friends sometime!

How can watches, minds and morals point to a Supreme Being? Write out your ideas to the following questions or statements:

How can a watch be an illustration of the reality of a Supreme Being?

_____

_____

Our minds point to the reality of a Supreme Being because _____

_____

_____

The fact that we have moral ideas of right and wrong demonstrates the reality of God because _____

_____

_____

Check out the following three examples and compare them with the answers you wrote above. (The first two examples will be given today. The third will be explored tomorrow.)

we live in a **designed** universe

Anglican clergyman William Paley argued in _Natural Theology_ . . . that a man chancing upon a watch in the wilderness could not conclude that the watch had simply always existed; rather, the obvious design of the watch – not only its internal makeup but also the fact that it clearly exists for a _purpose_ – would necessarily imply the existence of its designer. Paley went on to substitute the universe for the watch and contended that a mechanism so obviously designed as the universe necessitated the existence of a grand Designer (UTT, 50).

According to Paley, if a watch implies a "watchmaker," then a designed universe implies a _____.

A "Designer" capable of designing the entire universe would be "God." This "Designer/Creator/God" is not just a religious concept. The idea of a "Creator" is the most scientific conclusion that you can reach based on observations of the real world. Why is this true? _____

_____

_____

check it out!

Watches imply a watchmaker

we live in an **intelligent** universe

> Still another twist on the argument for the general revelation of God's existence is presented by C. S. Lewis. Suppose there were no intelligence behind the universe, says Lewis. In that case nobody designed my brain for the purpose of thinking. Thought is merely the by-product of some atoms within my skull. "But if so, how can I trust my own thinking to be true?" asks Lewis (UTT, 50).

Think about "thinking" for a moment. Are you thinking? Good. Now the very fact that you are "thinking" raises an important question: Where do your thoughts come from? (Pick the best answer)

- ☐ Electrical impulses between the synapses of the cells in my brain.
- ☐ I try not to think.
- ☐ Thinking gives me a headache.
- ☐ My mother told me never to think on days that start with "T" – Tuesday, Thursday, Today, Tomorrow, Taderday and Tunday!
- ☐ A mental/spiritual source.

Your mind is more that just your brain or the chemical processes of your "gray matter." Therefore, there must be more to reality than just our brains. There must be a God who created our minds to think true thoughts in order to comprehend God, the physical universe and ourselves.

Therefore, minds imply a Divine _____.

check it out!

Minds imply a Divine Intelligence

application time!

Read **Psalm 8**. In these nine verses the writer is praising God for the works of His hands. Meditate on these verses and turn the thoughts of the psalmist into your own words of praise. Enjoy!

_____

_____

_____

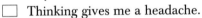

day 2 summary:

Like watches that imply a watchmaker, the universe implies a "universe maker" AND . . . minds imply a "Superior Mind".

more on watches, minds and morals
we live in a **moral universe**

There is a third line of thinking that directs us to the conclusion that God is real. Read on to find out what it is:

> C. E. M. Joad, who was an atheist for much of his professional career, wrote a book entitled *The Recovery of Belief* shortly before his death. This book traces his gradual advance toward God and Jesus Christ. Joad was largely convinced by his observation of human nature, his realization that a moral law exists, and that men often flaunt that law (UTT, 50).

What reason led this atheist to be convinced that God is real?

_____

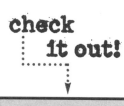

**check
it out!**

Morals imply a
moral law-giver

If there is no God, then the only foundation for building morals is a universe of molecules and energy. An impersonal universe is not a very promising source for ideas like "love one another" and "do not murder."

If naturalism were true, then saying that human actions were "bad" would make just as much sense as saying that a leaf blowing in the wind was "bad." How often have you done that?

But since we do have these ideals of love being good and murder being evil, there must be a moral, spiritual dimension from which these moral ideals flow. This moral agent is God, the ultimate source for moral ideals.

Therefore, morals imply a moral _____ - _____

the **God-connection**

There are three major characteristics of God:

        . . . **relational**
          . . . **ruler**
            . . . **righteous**

Which of the three "R's" relates to God's moral character?

   "God is R_____."

thinking like a christian

Look at the following verses and see how God's righteousness is reflected in his dealings with mankind:

> **Psalm 7:9 - O righteous God, who searches minds and hearts, bring to an end the violence of the wicked and make the righteous secure.**

> **Psalm 11:7 - For the LORD is righteous, he loves justice; upright men will see his face.**

Summarize these verses in your own words: _____ _____

_____

_____

There is also another side to God's righteousness. Read the following verses as you think about what they say about living a moral life:

> **Psalm 119:7-9 - I will praise you with an upright heart as I learn your righteous laws. I will obey your decrees; do not utterly forsake me. How can a young man keep his way pure? By living according to your word.**

How do God's righteous laws help us to know how to live?

_____

_____

the worldview connection

The following sentence is based on a summary of Joad's reasoning from human nature to God. Draw a line from each phrase to the worldview category that describes that concept:

C. E. M. Joad was a **seeker of truth**　　　　　　　**Theology**

who was studying **human nature**　　　　　　　　**Philosophy**

and came to realize that men were **moral creatures**　　　**Ethics**

which led to his conclusion that there must be a **God.**　　**Psychology**

It's amazing to see the connection between these different parts of the worldview puzzle. Someone can be **seeking truth** (Philosophy) by studying **human nature** (Psychology) and make observations about **morality** (Ethics) that lead to conclusions about the **existence and nature of God** (Theology).

Do you see how it all fits together to form a total view of reality? The Bible presents us with a coherent way of understanding ourselves and the world around us.

the life connection

Not only is God perfectly righteous in all His ways, but He distinguishes between good and evil in our behavior. Complete the verses printed below from **Proverbs 5:21-23:**

> For a man's ways are in _____ of the LORD, and he examines all his paths. The evil deeds of a wicked man _____ him; the cords of his sin hold him fast. He will die for lack of discipline, led astray by his own great _____.

There is a personal application in the Proverbs 5 passage. Describe in your own words the principle from these verses and how you can apply that principle to your life situation.

the principle:

_____

the application:

_____

day 3 summary:

The Bible clearly declares: GOD IS MORAL!

week 2 key verse: **Colossians 2:9 -**
"For in Christ all the fullness of the Deity lives in _____ form. . . "

who's to say what God is like?

There's another new student at school, a Hindu girl. After telling her your understanding of what God is like, she informs you that her view of God is quite different. In fact, she believes God is an impersonal cosmic energy that permeates everything in the entire universe.

You share with her how the universe displays the glory of God. (You had done your first days' assignment in your **journal**. Good for you)

She agrees, but says that if you take everything in the universe – the rocks, the trees, the dolphins, the asteroids, the stars, human life, etc. – and you blend them all together, then you have "god."

What would you say next to help your new friend understand that God is not the sum total of everything, but is a personal Being? (Hint: check your notes from "Day 2") _____

So, you explain that humans have a mind and this points to a personal God. Way to go! But then she says that our minds are just a part of the impersonal "cosmic consciousness" called "god." (Rats, where does she keep coming up with this stuff?)

What other line of evidence could you use to help her understand that God is real? (Don't forget about yesterday's study!) _____

Well, after you comment that within the heart of every person is a moral sense of what is right and wrong and that this means God is moral, you find that she actually agrees with you . . . sort of. She agrees that we must do what is good because otherwise we will be reincarnated as inferior animals to work off our bad "karma."

"Karma!" What's "karma?" You decide to drop the subject and rush off to your next class hoping that none of your friends saw you talking to her in the hall and ask about your conversation!

we've got a problem here

It seems that the universe is not too definite about the exact nature of God. Oh, sure, nature proclaims there is a God, but even someone of a different religion can appeal to nature and yet arrive at a conclusion about God that is very different from your own.

For the last two days we have looked at what can be known about God through **general revelation**, or the created order. But the question is: what characteristics of God can be gleaned from the natural world? As you think about that question, put a check mark by the qualities that you think can be known from observing creation:

"Maybe God is just a cosmic energy force."

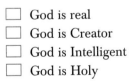

- ☐ God is real
- ☐ God is Creator
- ☐ God is Intelligent
- ☐ God is Holy
- ☐ God Judges Sin
- ☐ God Sent Jesus to Die for Man's Sin
- ☐ God is in Control of Everything
- ☐ God is Love

While the universe proclaims that **God is Real, Creator, Intelligent** and **Holy**, it is silent on what God is like beyond the attributes of power, intelligence and morality. The four qualities in the second column are not revealed to us through nature. The ideas of God's love, judgment, salvation and sovereignty are not understood by observing the world around us. We must find out about these attributes in another way.

The problem with **general revelation** is just that. . . it is too general! The Hindu student could appeal to nature to describe her idea of god just as you sought to use nature to defend your view.

But God has not left us to muddle through life with just a vague, general picture of Him. He has taken other steps to reveal to us a clear image of who He is and what He is like.

"A cosmic force doesn't communicate on a personal level."

special revelation **to the rescue**

> On the one hand, general revelation is God's communication of Himself to all persons, at all times, and in all places. Special revelation on the other hand, involves God's particular communications and manifestations which are available now only by consultation of certain sacred writings (UTT, 48).

Dig deeper into the description of **Special Revelation** by looking at each aspect of it:

What does "God's particular communications" mean?
For example, can you think of any of the many ways that God communicated to people in the past which are recorded in the Bible?

_____

_____

What does "manifestations" mean, and how is it different from God's "communications?"

_____

_____

How have God's past communications and manifestations been preserved for us?

_____

_____

Special Revelation involves God taking the initiative to communicate to mankind (that's the "revelation" part) through specific and particular ways (that's the "special" part). In the past, God revealed Himself by a number of different means: dreams, direct thoughts, direct encounters, even a burning bush! The authors of the Bible wrote down what God communicated to them so that we can read about it today.

What's so special about **Special Revelation**? It's specific! It gets down to the real details about who God is and His directions for our lives.

special revelation "reveals" God

To say that God is knowable is also to say that God "_____" or has personality–
that He is "_____." God's self-awareness, His emotions, and His self-determin-
ing will make up the core of His divine personality.

The Bible is emphatic in describing God as a person aware of Himself. In **Isaiah
44:6**, God says, **"I am the first and I am the last, and there is no God
besides me."** In **Exodus 3:14**, God says to Moses, **"I Am Who I Am."**

Remember the three major characteristics of God:

> . . . **relational**
> . . . **ruler**
> . . . **righteous**

Which of the three "R's" relates to God's desire to be intimately acquainted with His
creatures? **"God is R_____."**

check it out!

> To say that God is
> knowable is also to
> say that God "relates"
> or has personality —
> that He is personal.
> (UTT, 51)

relating to a personal God!

As you pray today, reflect on the fact that God is a personal Being who desires to
have a personal relationship with you.

day 4 summary:

> Through Special Revelation, the Bible, we discover the specifics about
> God's character.

# of ants and uncles and sons
an ant story from uncle ned

Uncle Ned used to tell the story about an anthill that was out by his barn. He would
tell it something like this:

> "Sometimes in the evening as the sun was starting to set, I would stroll out to the
> barn to check on the horses and enjoy the beauty of the sunset as it sprayed a
> golden glow across the wheat fields.

> One evening as I was leaning against the barn admiring the magnificent sunset, I
> happened to look down and noticed an anthill. I began to study the ants as they
> scurried around the ground in front of me. As I watched, one little ant crawled
> up onto my boot, ran across the toe and off the other side. I thought to myself,
> what a bold little fellow. He didn't even seem to realize that a being superior to
> himself existed. As I watched that little ant work, I wondered who put such
> boldness into so small a creature, and I wondered if I, too, was nothing more
> than just a little "ant."

Later on that summer, the weather got very hot and the fields became very dry. One afternoon, a thunderstorm hit our area. It came with lots of lightening but little rain. Suddenly, a flash of lightening hit the barn and it began to burn. Within seconds there was a raging fire. I hurried to get the animals out of the barn before it was too late. As I rounded the barn, I noticed the anthill and all the ants in their usual busy-ness. I thought, I hate to see those little guys fry from this fire, but there was no way that I could tell them of the impending danger to their home. If there was only some way that I could communicate to those creatures. But the only way that would happen would be for me to become like one of them. Then I could communicate to them in "ant" language.

What is the moral is this story? _____

_____

The most special thing about God's special revelation is that it involves a person. Jesus Christ was God's special message to mankind. He became one of us so that He could communicate to us in our language on a personal level.

God's son speaks our language

Yesterday, we discovered several lines of evidence that demonstrated that the Bible is inspired; it is from God. But there is another major reason for believing that the Bible is from God found in His most direct form of special revelation: Jesus Christ.

Complete the missing words from Hebrews 1:1-3:

> **In the past God _____ to our forefathers through the prophets at many times and in various ways, but in these last days he has spoken to us by his _____, whom he appointed heir of all things, and through whom he made the _____. The Son is the radiance of God's glory and the exact _____ of his being, sustaining all things by his powerful word. After he had provided _____ for sins, he sat down at the right hand of the Majesty in heaven.**

Christ is the "most special" Special Revelation of God.

If you want to know what God is like, look at Jesus. Jesus is the exact image or mirror of His Father.

Other "sacred" writings do not give a true picture of the world. Even though they may have some similarities with the moral teaching of Jesus, the writings of the Hindus, Muslims, and Buddhists contain many more differences from the Bible and the teachings of Jesus.

Only the Bible accurately describes the Christ as the image of God Himself.

Are you letting other people's ideas capture you by having doubts about Jesus being God? Yes / No

If you are not sure that Jesus is truly God, then you will have difficulty understanding other aspects of a Biblical worldview. A Biblical Christian view of life is founded on the Deity of Jesus Christ. He gives ultimate meaning of life.

application

check it out!

| Deity: (Latin) |
| Deos = God |

> **week 2** key verses: **Colossians 2:9-10**
> "For in _____ all the fullness of the Deity lives in bodily form and you have been given fullness in Christ, who is the head over every power and authority."

Take a few minutes to think about how Colossians 2:9-10 applies to you. How would believing this truth affect your relationship with

. . . God: _____

_____

. . . your parents/grandparents: _____

_____

. . . your brothers/sisters: _____

_____

. . . your friends: _____

_____

day 5 summary:

> The most special thing about God's Special Revelation is Jesus Christ.

week 2 summary:

The study of Theology asks the question: What about God? The Bible reveals that God is not playing hide-and-seek with us when it comes to knowing Him. Everything in the natural universe (General Revelation), everything in the Bible (Special Revelation) and everything about Jesus Christ makes it abundantly clear that God is ruler (He has all power), God is righteous (He is morally perfect), and God is relational (He loves us).

notes

thinking like a christian

philosophy
getting down to reality

> "Thinking is the hardest work there is, which is the probable reason why so few engage in it." – Henry Ford, 1929 (Quoted in *How to be Your Own Selfish Pig*, Susan Schaeffer Macaulay, p. 15)

Want to see your friends' eyes roll back into their heads? Ask them this question: "What is life all about?" Many people start rolling their eyes and open their mouths in a wide yawn when the subject of "philosophy" comes up. They say, "Get real!" What does philosophy have to do with LIFE?

Maybe you've even given a side-ways glance at the thought of such an impractical subject as philosophy. But actually, you and every one of your friends already have a philosophy, a way of understanding yourself and how you fit into the rest of the world. Yet, if you are like most people today, your philosophy is not thought out very clearly.

Philosophy is the starting point for everything else that you do. The way you react and behave always begins with the way you think about your life: that's your philosophy of life!

Therefore, if you want to GET REAL, philosophy will get you started by asking the question: **"What is real, and how do I know what is real?"** ◄ ················

This week, expect to

    . . . **be hungry for some real "wisdom"**

    . . . **understand that everybody believes in something**

    . . . **learn why the Bible is the source for "Truth"**

    . . . **make the connection between the reliability of the Scriptures and the resurrection of Jesus**

So don't just sit there rolling your eyes. Jump into the first day's session!

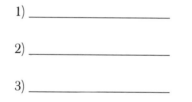

Question: What do you get when you cross a praying mantis and a termite?

Answer: A bug that says grace before eating your house.

It just goes to show that even a praying mantis can have a "worldview." He relates his theology to his everyday life!

Last week you discovered that what you believe about God is the basis of your worldview. This week you'll be discovering some really cool things about another worldview category. But before we mention the topic, the joke about a praying mantis makes me hungry. . . so let's talk about FOOD!

the three biggies

Everybody gets hungry. To satisfy that hunger you can order "BIGGIE" fries, a drink and a burger. While those three "biggies" may temporarily satisfy your desire for food, you know that in a few hours you will feel hungry again.

But food is not the only thing that we crave. All people crave the realization that their lives mean something. What would you say are the three BIG questions about life that most people crave to have answered?

1) _____

2) _____

3) _____

Speaking of questions, the three biggest questions many of your friends in school might have are "What's for lunch?", "When will this class be over?" and "Is this going to be on the test?".

So what are the **three big** questions in life? Most people will sooner or later ask the following:

   . . . **who am I?**
   . . . **why am I here?**
   . . . **where am I going?**

Do you realize that the way that you answer these three questions affects everything else in your life? And when you try to answer these "BIGGIES," you are treading the waters of what worldview category? _____

Perhaps you have not thought very much about your worldview, or philosophy of life. But one thing is sure; you have one, and you live it out everyday.

don't be taken captive!

> **week 2** key verse **Colossians 2:8** "See to it that no one takes you captive through hollow and deceptive philosophy, which depends on human tradition and the basic principles of this world rather than on Christ."

Look at this week's key verse. It warns against being taken _____ through the world's deceptive philosophies. What might be the results in a person's life if he or she were captured by a philosophy based on the principles of this world?

_____

_____

_____

understanding the times

The Bible records for us the story of a little band from the tribe of Issachar whose leaders had a unique perspective which brought them to David's aid. We are told that they "understood the times and knew what Israel should do" **(1 Chronicles 12:32).**

Because they had a clear understanding of the _____, they were able to take the right action. Their right beliefs led to right behavior!

In the same way, today, God is calling Christians to understand the culture of our times so we'll know what we need to do to not be captured by the world's philosophies such as naturalism, which say, "only nature exists."

food for thought

philosophy [Greek: philo (love) + sophia (wisdom)]: The love of wisdom; the attempt to discover an explanation for the whole of existence or reality. Philosophy involves seeking to know and understand the way the world is designed to work and then living according to that design.

If you are hungry, you will seek out something to eat, maybe a BIGGIE burger and fries. In a similar way, gaining wisdom starts with a hunger to understand what life is all about. Jesus said, "Blessed are they that hunger and thirst for righteousness..." **(Matthew 5:6).**

Spend the next few minutes reflecting on a portion of "wisdom" literature from the Bible, a chapter from the book of Proverbs. Use the space below to answer the following questions: What is the main point that the writer is making? What is the result if you follow the advice?

check it out!

1 Chronicles 12:32: " . . . men of Issachar, who understood the times and knew what Israel should do . . ."

week 3

thinking like a christian

proverbs 2

the main idea: (verses 1-6)

_____

_____

_____

the result in your life: (verses 9-10)

_____

_____

_____

day 1 summary:

There are three philosophical questions that everyone must answer: Who am I?, Why am I here?, and Where am I going?

week 3 day 2

ev'rbody's gotta believe sumfin
biology class blues

"Nature is all there is."

It's Monday morning, the first day of classes. You have Biology. As the bell rings, Mr. Matson clears his throat and begins:

This year in Biology we will be studying the world of living systems. During the course of our study, we will discuss the origins of life. These lessons will bring us to that subject that some of you dread, the "E" word: "evolution."

I know that a few of you in this class don't like to hear that word, but I can't help that. Evolution is the scientific theory that best explains the way that life arrived and developed on planet earth.

We are here to study scientific laws and theories. I don't want to hear any of your religious talk about God in this class!

You find yourself sinking further down into your seat and stealing sideways glances around the room. How do you feel right now? _____

nature is not naturalism!

"Nature" refers to the physical world that we can see and touch and measure. It's the world of molecules, mud and "mooo's." (As in "cow"–that was just to make sure you were still awake!)

thinking like a christian

But when you add the "ism" to the end of nature ("naturalism"), then it defines a way of thinking about the whole of reality. Naturalism is a worldview that _____ that _____ is all there is. Only stuff that you can touch and see is real. This means that there is no "supernatural" dimension to life.

supernaturalism and **reality**

On the other hand, "supernaturalism" is the philosophical view that there IS a reality that is different from the natural world. The conclusion from the group meeting was that there is a natural world AND a supernatural realm, and together, these two realms make up the **totality of reality**.

> The basic tenets of Christian philosophy can be demonstrated to be rational, for they are held by average, rational men and women. But surely, Christianity must still run into a. . . problem [regarding] how does the Christian "know" with out clashing with science and experience? How can the knowledge we gain through faith in Biblical revelation compare to knowledge gained by a scientific investigation of the universe? (UTT, 83)

How would you answer that last question: how does what we know through the Bible compare with what we know from science?

_____

_____

While some people today see a clash between the Bible and science, like the biology teacher at the beginning of this session, the biblical worldview maintains that there is _____ disagreement between true scientific discoveries and what the Bible teaches.

ev'rbody's got to assume sumfin!

> The basic problem of philosophy is not the old problem of faith versus reason. "The crucial problem," says Warren C. Young, "is that some thinkers place their trust in a set of assumptions in their search for truth, while other thinkers place their trust in a quite different set of assumptions." (UTT, 83-84)

So the clash is not between science and faith. It is a clash between "faith" in naturalism and "faith" in supernaturalism. Some people start with the belief (a faith assumption) that only nature is real. Christians start with the assumption that God is real.

However, some assumptions are better than others. So the issue is: which is the more reasonable assumption?

week 3

naturalism is a worldview that assumes that nature is ALL there is.

check it out!

There is NO disagreement between true scientific discoveries and what the Bible teaches.

Think back over your **journal** entries from last week. This idea of a supernatural Creator is not just a "blind" faith, but a reasonable, logical conclusion based on the facts of what we observe around us every day. Based on that evidence from the natural world, what do you think about Mr. Matson's approach to the study of science?

_____

_____

_____

_____

"But, Skip, aren't

you assuming

naturalism?"

apply it to your life!

Since God is real, it just makes sense to seek His wisdom not only about the natural universe but also how you should live. Turn to **Proverbs 2** and answer the following question as it is revealed in each of the verses indicated:

What are the benefits of seeking God's wisdom?

v. 11 - _____

v. 12 - _____

v. 16 - _____

v. 20 - _____

Close your time today by praying for God's wisdom about how you might share some of these ideas with your friends, or even your science teacher. Remember that a loving, gentle attitude is called for in situations like this.

day 2 summary:

A biblical philosophy supports a supernatural view of reality in contrast to the assumption of naturalism.

how do i know what's true?
two sources for **truth**

Yesterday we discovered two ways of looking at reality: naturalism and supernaturalism. So how do we decide which "ism" is the right "ism!" How do we know which one really describes reality?!

episte**what?!**

"Epistemology" is the fancy word used for answering the "how do I know" part of the question.

When you think about it, there are really only two sources for knowing what is true. What do you think those two sources would be?

#1 _____

#2 _____

Actually, you can either believe that truth comes from within yourself (self is the first option) or believe in a source outside of yourself (an outside source: the second option).

Why would the first option, "self," not be the best source for knowing ultimate truth?

_____

_____

That leaves the other option: an outside source. Which of the following would serve as an outside source for learning about what is true? Circle your answer:

A) Your pastor
B) Your parents
C) Your teachers
D) The Bible
E) A philosopher
F) Well-known literary works
G) A poet
H) A friend

Actually, any of the above could serve as a source for learning about reality. But for Christians which would be the best source? _____

whose sacred writings?

If you picked the Bible as the best source for understanding truth, you still have a problem here. Your Hindu friend at school says that her sacred writings are the right ones to follow. But Muslims also have their own sacred writings, and so do Buddhists. For that matter, the Mormons and Jehovah's Witnesses have their own versions of the Bible.

thinking like a christian

So what makes the Christian Bible so special? Why do Christians say that their sacred book is the right one? Can you think of any reasons for using the Bible as the source for truth instead of other sacred writings? List your thoughts:

1) _____

2) _____

3) _____

Circle any phrases in the textbox that give a reason for using the Bible as the source for knowing the truth.

> The evidence for the Christian's belief in the divine inspiration of the Bible is convincing. For example, the unity of teaching in the Bible is startling in light of the fact that its books were authored by different men faced with very different circumstances. Further, the astounding ability of the Bible to metamorphose the lives of individuals (for the better) who accept its authority strengthens its claim to be special revelation from God. The degree of moral truth contained in the Bible also supports its divine inspiration. All these arguments support the belief that the Bible is God's Word; however, the most convincing witness for divine inspiration is the Bible itself. Those hesitant to accept Scripture as God's special revelation are most often convinced by a thorough, open-minded study of the Bible (UTT, 48).

Use the phrases you circled and write them in your own words:

1) _____

2) _____

3) _____

4) _____

Which of the four reasons seems the most convincing to you? # ___
Why did you choose that one?

_____

_____

check it out!

"Inspiration" means "God — Breathed."

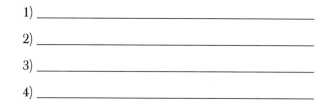

an **inspired** bible should **inspire** you to action

Look up 2 Timothy 3:16-17, and fill in the key words.

All Scripture is _____ and is useful for teaching, rebuking, correcting and training in _____, so that the man of God may be thoroughly _____ for every good work.

thinking like a christian

Write how these verses apply to your life.

_____

_____

_____

_____

day 3 summary:

Philosophy answers the question: How do I know what is true?

review key verse: **Colossians 2:8** See to it that no one takes you captive through hollow and deceptive philosophy, which depends on human tradition and the_____ _____ of this world rather than on Christ.

the bible: source for truth
reasons **to believe**

"You shouldn't question the Bible, should you?", Susan asked thoughtfully. "I mean, aren't we just supposed to believe what it says? But if that is so, why do I have so many questions? Why do I sometimes doubt if the Bible is true? I don't know if I can believe all those stories or not."

Susan is not alone in her questioning. She is expressing the thoughts of many people today. How would you answer her questions concerning the Bible?

_____

_____

tests for **truth**

Christian philosophy does not throw out reason or tests for truth. Christianity says the New Testament is true because its truths can be tested. [It considers] certain historical evidences that reason itself can employ as an attorney building a case uses evidences "in the law to determine questions of fact." Christian epistemology is based on special revelation, which in turn is based on history, the law of evidence, and the science of archaeology (UTT, 84).

check it out!

Epistemology: the study of how we know what we know

The above paragraph describes Christian **epistemology** as being based on S_____ R_____. What are three reasons mentioned above that demonstrate the Bible is true?

1) _____

2) _____

3) _____

First, the **historical evidence.**

what if . . .

. . . you took 40 different people...living in different places...at different times (war & peace)...writing in different moods (from joy to sorrow)...coming from three different continents...writing in three different languages about many controversial topics. . . and if you put all of their writings together, what would you expect to have? (Check your answer)

☐ a unified, harmonious story
☐ a disjointed series of different ideas

Did you know that the Bible was written in just that way? It was written (fill in the blanks from the above "What if" paragraph)

...by 40 different _____: solders, shepherds, statesmen, common men, and kings,

...by men living in different _____: the desert, the palace, small towns, large cities,

...at different _____: periods of war and times of peace; times of prosperity and times of need,

...in different _____: feelings of great joy and of great sorrow; moments of fear and times of security,

...from three different _____: in Egypt, in Italy, in Judea,

...in three different _____: Hebrew, Greek and Aramaic,

...about many controversial _____: the nature of God, moral issues, political alliances, religious ceremonies,

... yet the Bible is not a mix of contradictory ideas. It reads like one story with harmony and continuity from Genesis to Revelation.

Write your conclusion based on the above historical evidence about how the Bible was written: _____

_____

_____

The historical evidence demonstrates that the Bible is unique = one of a kind. It is different from any other religious writing in the way that it was written.

the Bible is **true** for you

Another part of the Bible's uniqueness is its ability to change the lives of those who read and obey it. Read the following verses and write down the instruction given and the benefit you receive for following that wise advise:

Proverbs 3:

    v. 1-2 - Wise advice: _____

       Personal benefit: _____

    v. 3-4 - Wise advice: _____

       Personal benefit: _____

day 4 summary:

> The "historical test" examines how the Bible was written by different people over time and demonstrates that the Bible is unique — one of a kind, different from all other religious writings.

the bible: history and his story

the bible before the court of **legal evidence**

Legal evidence refers to the principles that apply in a court of law. To verify if a crime took place at a particular time in the past, what types of evidences might be used in court?

_____

_____

One of the best kinds of evidence is eye-witness testimony. But even eye-witnesses must be evaluated as to their reliability.

43

thinking like a christian

is the bible reliable?

The original documents of the Bible are no longer around. How do we know that valuable information has not been lost in the translations handed down from generation to generation?

When dealing with any ancient document such as the Bible, researchers evaluate two things:

#1: what is the time-interval between the original work and our earliest copy? First they date the copies that they actually have in hand to determine how long it has been from the original writing.

Why would this be important to evaluate?

_____

#2: how many copies do we have? Second, researchers evaluate the total number of copies available.

Why would this be important?

_____

"There's a difference between believing

the evidence

This type of information is called **"Bibliographic"** evidence. Let's compare the New Testament with some other works of antiquity.

1) Caesar wrote a history of the Gallic wars around 58-50 B.C. There are only 9 or 10 good copies, the oldest being 900 years later than Caesar's day.

2) Livy's history of Rome was written from 59 B.C. to A.D. 17. We only have 20 partial manuscript copies, with only one dating within 400 years of the original.

3) For the **New Testament**, there are over 14,000 manuscript copies, some within just 250 - 300 years after the original documents were written with fragments as early as 100-150 years!

Write a conclusion in your own words based on the legal evidence:

_____

_____

ANYTHING and believing the RIGHT thing!"

The scholar John Warwick Montgomery concludes: "to be skeptical of the resultant text of the New Testament books is to allow all of classical antiquity to slip into obscurity, for no documents of the ancient period are as well attested bibliographically as the New Testament."[1]

thinking like a christian

the **resurrection** factor

In court, eyewitness testimony is important. How does this relate to the Bible?

Paul wrote that the resurrection was proof positive that Jesus was the true Son of God. Look up **1 Corinthians 15:1-7.** Notice the references to real people that saw Jesus alive after His crucifixion. Make a list of those people:

_____

_____

_____

_____

This kind of evidence would stand up in any court of law.   The historical and legal evidence leads to the conclusion that Jesus actually was raised from the dead. And if this is true, then we need to pay attention to what Jesus had to say about what's important in life.

Do you have any reason to doubt what the Bible says? If you still have some lingering doubts concerning the reliability of the Bible, write your questions here and talk them over with your Bible study leader or pastor this week:

_____

_____

_____

day 5 summary:

The Bibliographic test confirms that the Bible has some of the best evidence for its reliability compared with other ancient documents.

the **world of ideas** alert:

If you haven't done so this week, take a few minutes to look in the newspaper for any articles that relate to the "World of Ideas," and bring them to the next group meeting.

review key verse: **Colossians 2:8** "See to it that no one takes you captive through hollow and deceptive philosophy, which depends on human tradition and the basic principles of this world rather than on _____."

45

thinking like a christian

week 3 summary:

Philosophy asks the questions: What is real, and how do I know? The biblical worldview states that reality consists of both the natural universe and the supernatural realm. Because the evidences for the reliability of the Bible are convincing, we can conclude that what the Bible says about the source of wisdom and knowledge (Colossians 2:2-3) is true and draw principles for true beliefs and wise living based on what the Bible teaches.

ENDNOTES
[1] *History and Christianity*, John W. Montgomery, Downers Grove, IL.: InterVarsity Press, 1971, p.29.

is it "creation" or "evolution"

For the past 130 years the issue of "creation and evolution" has been a hotly debated topic from high school biology classrooms to U.S. and state supreme courts. What's a Christian student to think in light of the conflicting arguments? Some resort to arguing when the subject of evolution comes up. Others buy into the idea of evolution and begin to doubt the biblical account of creation. Still others throw up their hands with a "Who cares?!" attitude.

What you believe about the origin of life does matter. It determines not only how you think about biology, but also how you think about every other worldview category. For example, your view on the origin of human life has significant implications for how you understand basic human psychology. Are we a little "higher" than the apes (according to evolutionary theory) or a little "lower" than the angels (according to Psalm 8:5)?

During this week your journey will take you into the biblical worldview of "special creation." You will explore the following areas:

- the difference between evolutionary theory and creation ◄·······················

- the foundation for modern science is the biblical worldview

- how the two basic principles of evolution do not validate evolutionary theory

- why an Intelligent Designer (God) is the only scientifically possible solution to the origin-of-life debate

While this week's study may not answer all of your questions concerning the origins debate, it will lay the foundation for further study based on a solid biblical worldview.

---

week 4 key verses: **Colossians 1:16-17**
"For by [Christ] all things were created: things in heaven and on earth, visible and invisible, whether thrones or powers or rulers or authorities; all things were created by him and for him. He is before all things, and in him all things hold together."

---

creation or evolution?
what does it matter?

It's the first day of the new school year. As you are walking out of biology class, your friend pulls up beside you in the hall and says,

> Mr. Matson was really onto that "evolution" and "creation" thing today in class. I don't see what the big problem is. What does it matter what you think about how life originated? Can't we just study plants and animals and not worry about how they got here? What difference does it make if God created life or if life started all by itself in some "primordial soup" billions of year ago?

How would you respond to your friend? Does it matter what you believe about the origin of life? Explain your answer: _____

_____

_____

check it out!

The theory of evolution states that all life came about by impersonal forces operating by chance over 3.5 billions of years without any intervention from God.

Evolutionary theory assumes that life originated from _____ forces (mutation and natural selection) operating by _____ without any intervention from _____.

It matters a lot what you believe about the origin of life because it relates directly to what you believe about other areas. If evolution is true, what are the implications concerning each of the following areas:

God:

_____

_____

Human nature:

_____

_____

Moral standards:

_____

_____

what difference does it make?

If evolution is true, then God has nothing to do with the origin of life. Nature did not need His help in bringing about life and all the different types of plants and animals living today. Therefore, the idea of "God" is simply a concept that primitive man developed to try to understand the mysteries of life.

As far as human nature is concerned, evolution describes mankind as the highest form of living organism. This assumes that we are basically good and getting better all the time. There is no sin problem marring our basic instincts.

And related to moral standards, evolutionary theory concludes that these are just social ideas that have come about over time and are constantly changing and "evolving" to fit the evolutionary progress of the human species. Morals are whatever you want them to be: they are relative and situational.

How does this view contrast with a biblical perspective?

_____

_____

but what about . . .

But some Christians object to the above implications of evolution by saying that God could have used the process of evolution to bring about life. This is called theistic evolution.

Theistic evolutionists contend that the term "creation" simply means that God created the first spark of life and then _____ His creation through the vehicle of _____.

What's wrong with that? Hint: Jacques Monod and Bertrand Russell, both evolutionists, refer to evolution as a wasteful, cruel process (elimination of the weakest species, etc.). Is this a picture of the God of the Bible (see Genesis 1:31; John 1:1-3)?

_____

_____

_____

check it out!

Theistic evolutionists contend that the term creation simply means that God created the first spark of life and then directed His creation through the vehicle of evolution.

week 4

the worldview connection

What's wrong with theistic evolution? It tries to mix two different worldviews. The biblical worldview has definite implications about the origin of life based on its belief about God (theology), an understanding about mankind (psychology) and a view of what is moral (ethical). Once you begin to see the connections between these seemingly different categories, you are thinking in terms of a total worldview.

But evolutionary theory has implications in these same areas, only with vastly different conclusions because the theory of evolution is based on a different worldview from that of the Bible.

People who believe in evolution begin with a different set of assumptions. Their philosophical starting point is called naturalism. (Refer to week 3, day 2 for what was said about naturalism.) This worldview assumes that there is no God (their theology) and that the totality of reality is just the material universe, there is no supernatural (their philosophy). Based on these beliefs; theories in science are constructed.

theological differences

The two views of origins also have very different implications concerning the nature of mankind.

> More important, if evolution is true, then the story of the Garden of Eden and original sin must be viewed as nothing more than allegory, a view that undermines the significance of Christ's sinless life and sacrificial death on the cross. . . . If Adam was not a historical individual, and if his fall into sin was not historical, then the Biblical doctrines of sin and of Christ's atonement for it collapse (UTT, 152-153).

In your own words state the problem presented above:

_____

_____

reflecting on God's creation

Spend a few minutes reading Psalm 19:1-6. Then, pause and thank God for his power in creating the beauty of this world and for how God has provided a consistent worldview.

day 1 summary:

What you believe about the origin of life matters!

science and religion
things that go together

Chocolate chip cookies and ice-cold milk—a great combination! They just naturally go together. List three other pairs that go together:

1) _____

2) _____

3) _____

Summertime and vacations, Thanksgiving and turkey, fall Fridays and football. We make a connection between each pair because we are accustomed to having them in combination.

But what about science and religion? Do they "go together"? Many people consider these two fields of study totally incompatible.

modern science and the bible

Modern science's roots are grounded in a Christian view of the world. This is not surprising, since science is based on the assumption that the universe is orderly and can be expected to act according to specific, discoverable laws. An ordered, lawful universe would seem to be the effect of an intelligent Cause, which was precisely the belief of many early scientists (UTT, 153).

What does this say about the religious foundation of modern science?

_____

_____

What is it about Biblical Christianity that forms the basis for studying the world of nature?

_____

_____

founders of modern science

Do religion and science go together? The early "modern" scientists lived in the 1600's and founded the principles of science that we still use today. Read what some of them had to say on the subject of religion and science.

Johannes Kepler (1571-1630) is the founder of modern astronomy. He demonstrated that the sun is the center of the solar system, published the first tables for tracking star motions, and contributed to the development of calculus.

He stated that in his scientific research he was merely "thinking God's thoughts after Him." **What do you think Kepler meant by that phrase?**

_____

_____

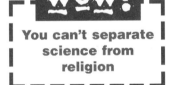

wow!

You can't separate
science from
religion

Robert Boyle (1627-1691) is credited with being the father of modern chemistry. He was also a diligent student of the Bible and devoted much of his own money to Bible translation.

Do you imagine that Boyle saw a problem between his study of chemistry and his belief in God? Why not?

_____

_____

Isaac Newton (1642-1727) discovered the law of universal gravitation, formulated the three laws of motion, and developed calculus into a comprehensive branch of mathematics. As an astronomer, he constructed the first reflecting telescope. He wrote many books on Biblical subjects as well as papers refuting atheism and defending creation and the Bible. Regarding the solar system, Newton wrote:

> This most beautiful system of sun, planets, and comets could only proceed from the counsel and dominion of an intelligent and powerful Being.[1]

Did Newton's strong belief in God help or hinder his ability to be involved in useful scientific inquiry and discovery?

_____

_____

Based on the above comments from the most influential early modern scientists, write a brief summary concerning how science and religion interface.

_____

_____

_____

search for "the world of ideas"

Take a few minutes to search the newspaper or your biology textbook to look for signs of "intelligent life" on planet earth.

Bring an article or idea to the next group meeting and share with everyone its worldview.

day 2 summary:

Modern science was born out of a biblical worldview and presents no conflict between true science and the Bible.

modern science and creation
living in the 21st century

After telling your friend what you know about the early modern scientists and their biblical worldview, your friend responds,

> Sure, that may have been true for those guys back 300 years ago, but face it, science has discovered a lot since then. We no longer need "God" to

explain how things work. Science has demonstrated that life could develop and evolve on its own without His help.

Your friend has a point. Is the worldview of the early scientists still valid today? Is there evidence of design and a Designer, or have we gained new knowledge that would allow us to reject the Biblical view of a Creator? What do you think?

_____

_____

relearning old lessons

> Science is re-learning an old lesson: the more one discovers about the universe, the more one discovers design. Many notable scientists . . . describe the design in nature revealed to them through science. Physicist Paul Davies, who does not profess to be a Christian, supports. . . creationism when he says, "Every advance in fundamental physics seems to uncover yet another facet of order." At first, this seems to be an obvious conclusion of little significance. But strict evolution demands chance rather than a Law-maker as the guiding force. When a world-class non-Christian scientist like Davies declares that the universe cannot be viewed as a product of chance, it is a severe blow to materialistic evolutionary theory (UTT, 154).

What is the point that world-class physicist Paul Davies makes?

_____

_____

How does this contradict strict evolutionary theory?

_____

_____

Not only did the early modern scientists believe in a Creator of life and the cosmos, many of the top scientists in our own generation believe the same thing. To get an idea of how some of the best scientists of today relate religion and science, check out the following quotes:

modern scientists

Wernher von Braun (1912-1977) was one of the world's top space scientists. A leading German rocket engineer, he migrated to the United States and became Director of NASA. He wrote:

Manned space flight is an amazing achievement, but it has opened for

mankind thus far only a tiny door for viewing the awesome reaches of space. An outlook through this peephole at the vast mysteries of the universe should only confirm our belief in the certainty of its Creator. I find it ... difficult to understand a scientist who does not acknowledge the presence of a superior rationality behind the existence of the universe...[2]

What did viewing the "vast mysteries of the universe" lead von Braun to conclude about the existence of God?

_____

_____

Professor Henry Margenau, professor of physics for over 40 years at Yale University, has received 8 honorary doctorate degrees, was a visiting professor at 12 universities, and worked with Albert Einstein. He said:

If you ask scientists who have a mild training in science...you do get the impression that there is a conflict between science and religion. But if you ask really good scientists...leading scientists, the people who have made contributions which have made science grow so vastly in the last fifty years, [these scientists] are... all religious in their beliefs.[3]

Based on Professor Margenau's comment, the "really good" top scientists around the world see science and religion as having:

- ☐ some conflict
- ☐ a lot of conflict
- ☐ no conflict

There are many other current scientists who could be quoted, but you get the idea from these that there is no basic conflict between the study of science and Biblical Christianity.

reality and rationality

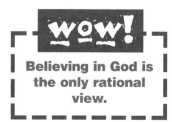

Phillip Johnson, professor of law at U.C. Berkley, stated in his book, *Reason in the Balance*:

If God really does exist, then to lead a rational life a person has to take account of God and his purposes. A person or a society that ignores the Creator is ignoring the most important part of reality, and to ignore reality is to be irrational.[4]

Read Psalm 19:1-5. The writer of this psalm made the rational connection between the Creator and the creation. Reflect on its meaning for you and our society as you put your thoughts in writing:

_____

_____

day 3 summary:

Because of the abundant evidence that the universe is "designed," many modern scientists rationally conclude that there is a Grand Designer.

> **review** key verses: **Colossians 1:16-17**
> "For by [Christ] all things were created: things in heaven and on earth, visible and invisible, whether thrones or powers or rulers or authorities; all things were created ____ ____ and ____ ____. He is before all things, and in him all things hold together."

in the "big inning" or in the "beginning . . .?"
spontaneous generation

"O.K., O.K., so there are some scientists today who believe that God has something to do with science and the origin of life," your friend acknowledges as the two of you are making your way out to the parking lot after class. "But it says right here in our biology textbook on page 199 that 'most scientists think that life arose on Earth from inanimate matter'. . ."

Your friend continues, "And then on the next page the biology text even shows an experiment by Stanley Miller which demonstrated how the building blocks of life could have formed spontaneously on the early earth. It seems that these experiments prove that life could come about without the help of some supernatural Being."

How would you respond to your friend's comments:

_____

_____

Most high school and college textbooks give only the positive aspects of the above Miller experiment, leaving out any negative data. So for the sake of fairness and honest scientific inquiry, let's see if there is any contrary information concerning these types of experiments.

in the "big inning"

First of all, you need to keep in mind that origin-of-life experiments are supposed to be re-enactments of what could have happened in a warm pond on the early earth. But scientists manipulate the experiment in different ways to get the desired results. How is this done? Let's compare the Miller experiment to a baseball team. It's the bottom of the ninth, the game is tied, and the best "origin-of-life" batter comes to the plate. This is the "Big Inning!"

the first pitch: All chemists know that in a real pond there would be all sorts of chemical reactions, many that would cancel out the reactions needed for the formation of life. So what does the researcher do? He starts with pure ingredients. But in a natural setting, there is no way to purify the starting materials to get the results you want. The "origin of life" batter just swung and missed: "Strike one!"

the second pitch: All good chemists also know that ultraviolet light from the sun destroys amino acids (the building blocks of life). So in these origin-of-life experiments the scientist screens out certain wavelengths of light. However, in a natural setting there would be no "filter" to remove these deadly rays. That's "Strike two!" against the odds of life originating by itself.

the third pitch: A third thing that scientists know is that the building blocks of life (amino acids and proteins) are very delicate and can easily break down into the original chemicals that make them up. So the researcher rigs a trap to remove them from the reaction site as soon as they form, to protect them from disintegration. But nature doesn't come with protective traps. In real life, any amino acids that form quickly disintegrate. So the experiment misses real life again: "Strike three!"

The umpire looks at the origin-of-life batter and hollers,
"You're out!"

Actually, the origin-of-life experiments have eleven major problems, the three just mentioned plus eight more! Any one of these eleven problems by itself would stop the progress from non-living molecules to living cells.

Based on the above "batting average," what can you say concerning the idea of "spontaneous generation":

_____

_____

_____

_____

Origin-of-life experiments have eleven major problems.

God hits a homerun

> Dean Kenyon, a biochemist and a former chemical evolutionist, now writes, "When all relevant lines of evidence are taken into account, and all the problems squarely faced, I think we must conclude that life owes its inception to a source outside of nature" (UTT, 156).

Professor Dean Kenyon co-authored a popular college textbook on chemistry, so he should know something about the origin of life. Dr. Kenyon concludes that the evidence points to life coming from . . .

- ☐ a warm pond + natural processes
- ☐ another planet
- ☐ a supernatural source

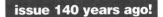

"life only comes from . . ."

Take the same biology textbook your friend was using and look back a couple of chapters. You will find that this idea of where life comes from was decided scientifically in 1860, the year after Darwin published his theory on evolution.

For hundreds of years, people thought that life could generate itself from non-living matter. They pointed to such things as frogs emerging from the mud of riverbanks as evidence for this idea.

But in 1860, Louis Pasteur ended the controversy by a series of scientific experiments, proving that "life only comes from pre-existing life." His experiments have been verified over the years and <u>never</u> contradicted.

How does Pasteur's scientific conclusion compare with current evolutionary theory? You could chart it this way:

science says . . .   **evolution says . . .**

"Life comes from life"   "Life comes from non-life"

Now, put on your scientist's thinking cap and evaluate those two statements by answering the following questions:

What do you notice as you compare these two statements?

_____

Which statement has been proven scientifically to be true?

_____

Since the two statements are contradictory, then if one is true, what would the other be?   A) True   B) False

thinking like a christian

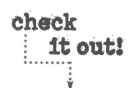

"If a high-school curriculum incorporates the subject of biological origins, and if supernatural creation is a rational alternative to naturalistic evolution within that subject, then it is bad educational policy as well as viewpoint discrimination to try to keep students ignorant of an alternative that may be true."
- Professor of Law, Phillip E. Johnson, *Reason in the Balance*, 1995, p. 26.

Don't miss this point: the most basic premise of evolution, the idea that "life comes from non-life," is scientifically a false statement!

If "evolution" is not based on scientific observations, then what is it? Evolution is based on naturalism, which is a religious assumption we explored on Week 3, Day 2. In contrast, the biblical worldview states what science has verified to be true: "life only comes from life!"

Read **Genesis 1:11, 20** and **2:7** to find out the most scientifically accurate statement you can make regarding the origin of life: "In the beginning, _____ _____ ..."

day 4 summary:

Concerning the origin of life, "life comes from life" has been scientifically demonstrated to be true, confirming the biblical worldview of a Creator!

"after their kind . . ."
what do corn, cows and cats prove?

Your friend and biology lab partner is sure persistent. He is convinced that science has proven evolution to be true.

After talking with him about the problems with the origin-of-life experiments, he changes the subject: "But look at all of the evidence for evolution. I mean, take 'natural selection' for example. Scientists have done breeding experiments to produce sweeter corn and cows that give more milk and cats with fluffier fur. If a breeder can select for certain traits, then nature can select to produce changes for the better. So natural selection proves evolution!"

Your friend has a point. How do you respond to his argument for natural selection creating new species?

_____

_____

bird's beaks and evolution?

When Darwin made his famous voyage to the Galapagos Islands, he discovered on the various islands finches that differed slightly in the size of their beaks. He thought he had discovered evolution in action. But had he?

Darwin's theory of evolution assumes that all of the diversity of life in the world today came from simpler, less complex forms of life. You might call it the "amoeba to man" theory.

For this "amoeba to man" idea to actually work, new structures must emerge. Let's face it, a man is much more complex than an amoeba!

For evolution to take place you have to _____ ____ _____.

For evolution to occur, you must "add new stuff"!

Now let's evaluate Darwin's observations concerning the finches:
Did he observe any "new stuff" being added to the birds?   (Yes / No)

What did he observe? _____

Darwin only observed small changes in the size of the finches beaks, not the addition of new features. What Darwin noticed was "adaptation," the process where animals can change slightly to "adapt" to their environment. But these small adaptive changes have never been observed to lead to whole new structures.

The same thing is true for other examples given in most biology textbooks. The famous "peppered moth" example begins with moths and ends with moths, no new features were ever added! This is adaptation but not evolution!

creator to the rescue

Turn to **Genesis 1:12, 21, 25** and you will notice that God creates various plants and animals "according to their _____."

A biblical "kind" is an inter-breeding group.

The phrase "after its kind" suggests that the boundary between kinds is defined by reproduction: a "kind" is an _____ - _____ group.

For example, the entire cat family, from domestic cats to leopards and tigers, forms a breeding chain and hence constitutes a single "kind." So does the dog family, from our friendly beagles to wolves and even jackals.

"When you can grow wings on pigs, then I'll believe in evolution!"

wings on pigs!

Edward Deevey, Jr [has written] "Some remarkable things have been done by crossbreeding and selection inside the species barrier, or within a larger circle of closely related species, such as the wheats. But wheat is still wheat, and not, for instance, grapefruit; and we can no more grow wings on pigs than hens can make cylindrical eggs" (UTT, 158).

Does natural selection prove evolution? Write your conclusion regarding the concept of natural selection based on the best scientific observations:

_____

_____

evolution, creation and faith

> The belief that God created all things, including man in His own image, requires faith. But evolutionary theory requires more faith, since evolution runs contrary to reason, science and history (UTT, 162).

What is the difference between faith in a Creator and faith in evolution?

_____

_____

Review each day's assignment for this week. Which ideas were most significant to you? Why?

_____

_____

Spend some time in praise to God for His awesome power and wisdom in creating this diverse world of beautiful living things.

day 5 summary:

Evolution assumes that plants and animals can "add new stuff" over time, but this has never been observed to happen, confirming the need for a Creator.

week 4 summary:

How you view the origin of life matters! An unbiased study of biology leads to the following conclusions:

1) living organisms show incredible evidence of "design,"
2) life only comes from pre-existing life, and
3) living things reproduce only after their own kind.

The most scientific statement you can make concerning the origin of life is: "In the beginning God created . . ."!

action point:

Invite a group of your friends over for pizza and a discussion of the ideas from this week's study on biology. It will help them think through the issues and evaluate what they hear in biology class. And if they are not Christians, it will demonstrate the logical basis for believing in God and Jesus Christ. Pray about it and **go for it!**

ENDNOTES

[1] Cited in *The Soul of Science*, Nancy R. Pearcey and Charles B. Thaxton, Crossway Books, Wheaton, IL., 1994, p.91.
[2] *Men of Science, Men of God*, Henry M. Morris, Master Books, 1988: p.85.
[3] *The Intellectuals Speak Out About God*, Roy Varghese, Regnery Gateway, Inc., 1984: p. 43.
[4] *Reason in the Balance*, Phillip E. Johnson, a professor of law at U.C. Berkeley, p. 7.

 **psychology**

how to live with yourself and like it

Let's face it, you do all of your living in your head. It's the thoughts that you have every minute of every day that keep you doing the things you do. You think, "I'm hungry!", so you go to the refrigerator to look for something to eat. You think, "I'm lonely!", so you call a friend and talk for two hours. You think, "I'm . . ." —you get the point.

The ideas you have about life determine how much you enjoy life. Are you happy and satisfied with your life? It's because you think that way. Are you sad and depressed? Often those feelings stem from the way you think about yourself.

So what is the source of your thoughts and ideas? When it comes right down to it, who are "YOU"?!

To find out the answer to those questions, we turn to "Psychology"–the study of the "psyche," or "soul." Psychology tries to understand what you are like on the inside, the place where you do all of your real living. In other words, psychology is the study of the basic nature of people.

During this week's journey you will discover

 . . . **the biblical view of "YOU"!** ◄

 . . . why you don't have to put on an "act" around parents and friends

 . . . your royal heritage as a Christian, and

 . . . how <u>not</u> to be your own selfish pig!

So to enjoy life to the max, start with a new set of ideas from your study of Biblical Christian psychology!

---

week 5 key verse: **Colossians 2:13**
"When you were dead in your sins and in the uncircumcision of your sinful nature, God made you alive with Christ. He forgave us all our sins . . ."

---

who am i, really?
psychology, the bible, and you

"You're just a cosmic accident, so get used to it!"

Ever ask yourself the question: "Who am I, really?" Good question. Read on for some really good biblical answers.

Psychology is the study of what makes up the real "you" on the inside. The Bible has a lot to say about who you really are.

> Christianity and psychology are compatible for the simple reason that the world view of Biblical Christianity contains a psychology. As Charles L. Allen aptly points out, "the very essence of religion is to adjust the mind and soul of man. . . . Healing means bringing the person into a right relationship with the physical, mental and spiritual laws of God." Man created "in the image of God" (Genesis 1:27) requires a worldview that recognizes the significance of the spiritual (UTT, 192).

There's an interesting connection between the study of psychology and the other worldview categories that we have discussed so far. Match each phrase with the worldview category related to it by drawing a line between the two:

"religion"   **psychology**

"Mind and soul of man"   **theology**

"physical, mental and spiritual laws of God"   **biology**

"created"   **philosophy**

The big idea that is emerging from our study is this: there is a connection between each of the worldview categories. The Bible builds a whole picture of LIFE, even how you view yourself.

the bible's view of you

Walk into almost any high school or college psychology class and you will be taught that "you" are just a bundle of molecules and electrical impulses. This is called "psychological monism"–referring to a "one-dimensional" view of humankind based on atheistic theology, naturalistic philosophy and evolutionary biology.

However, the Bible reveals a different understanding of man's basic make-up.

Find the following passage and answer the questions:

Matthew 10:28:

Who is speaking? (see verse 5) _____

What two dimensions of life does Jesus refer to? _____

_____

What does Jesus say about our bodies? _____

_____

What does he say about our souls? _____

What evidence do you see that people consist of a spiritual dimension? (Hint: Ideas and beliefs are not physical entities.)

_____

_____

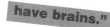

"Explain to me how cosmic accidents have brains."

dualism . . . no kidding!

"You" are more than just your physical body. And "you" are more than just a product of natural processes operating over time.

> The Bible's statements regarding body, breath of life, soul, spirit, and mind suggest a dualist ontology; that is, the view that human nature consists of two fundamental kinds of reality: physical (material or natural) and spiritual (supernatural) . . . The Bible does not deny body; it simply says man is more than body (UTT, 192).

According to the biblical view, the real "you" consists of . . .

    . . . a _____ (bones and blood and skin), plus
    . . . a _____ (a special and unique personality)

So, you're pretty special after all!

wow!

A Biblical View of "You"
You = Body + Soul

time to celebrate!

Your body is not the only part of you, or even the most important part of you. The "real" you, the part that lasts forever, is on the inside of this wonderful body.

Take a few minutes to celebrate the real "you." Make a list of the special qualities that God has given you in each area:

body: _____

soul: _____

. . . and don't forget to thank God for making you so special!

day 1 summary:

Celebrate the real you: body and soul.

thinking like a christian

self esteem and the bible
kathy's world

It really shattered my life when my parents' marriage broke up, she began. I was thirteen, and I couldn't get it out of my head that somehow I was responsible for the breakup. Everybody had been so grouchy and disapproving of me for so long that I figured it all must be my fault. . .

As I went through school, I was very mixed up. I felt unsure of myself, so I tried to do anything that I thought would get other kids to accept me. If they were smoking, I'd smoke. If a boy wanted something sexual from me, I'd give in. When drugs were passed out, I'd try them. All the time I was really crying, "Am I worth anything to anybody?"[1]

No one would have guessed that Kathy felt this way. On the outside she was full of fun. But under that external veneer of joy and energy was a deep-seated inner despair.

Do you know someone like Kathy? _____

Have you ever had some of the same feelings as Kathy's? If so which ones?

_____

Kathy seems to have a problem that goes beyond her parents' divorce.
What would that problem be?_____

_____

Could it be that Kathy wanted to matter as a person, but she had no basic reason for believing that she did? Maybe she had bought into the logical conclusion of an evolutionary worldview that told her that she was just another human animal on the planet for a few years–just a mobile, talking hunk of dust.

Kathy cried out, "Am I worth anything to anybody?" If she had said that to you, what would you have said in reply?

_____

_____

_____

the truest things about you

Kathy was feeling depressed because she believed she lived in a one-dimensional universe. All she could see was the physical world, the natural realm of existence, her "outer shell." So when her world started to cave in around her, she was left without any means of coping with her feelings of isolation and abandonment.

thinking like a christian

We learned during our study of Biblical Philosophy that our universe is not one-dimensional, but two-dimensional. What are the two realms that make up the **"totality of reality"**?

       1) The N_____ realm

       2) The S_____ realm

check it out!

The "Totality of Reality" is the natural *and* the supernatural.

> Man's spiritual element is his very essence and the element of man that proper psychology should focus upon. A psychology that ignores the existence of the spirit cannot hope to deal with the deepest, most profound problems experienced by man (UTT, Unabridged Version, 409).

Secular Humanist psychologists ignore the spiritual dimension of life when it comes to dealing with people's personal problems. What are some of the results of this denial?

_____

_____

God's image / my image

In contrast to Secular Humanist psychology, check out what God says about humanity. After each passage, apply the idea to Kathy's life by writing out what you would tell her about who she really is.

passage   **main idea**   **applied to kathy**

Genesis 1:27 -

Psalm 8:4-5 -

Psalm 139:13-14 -

Psalm 139:15-16 -

All of these passages deal with a very important idea. How would you summarize that idea?_____

_____

What makes you so special is that God has made you in His image. God's image is not found in your body or physical being, but in your mental, moral and spiritual capabilities.

wow!

A positive self-image comes from your God-image.

true self esteem

Self esteem is not produced by just thinking warm fuzzy things about yourself. It comes as a result of understanding who you really are. And the truest thing about you is what God says about you!

Take another look at those passages that you applied to Kathy's life. Guess what? They apply to your life, too! After each passage, write how the main idea relates to you.

who am I, really!

Genesis 1:27 - _____

Psalm 8:4-5 - _____

Psalm 139:13-14 - _____

Psalm 139:15-16 - _____

day 2 summary:

> Self esteem grows as you gain a right view of you: specially created in God's image.

greatly fallen
kathy's acting career

Kathy felt mixed up and unsure of herself, so she turned to acting, pretending to be somebody that she is not. Read how she describes it. . .

> . . . I tried to do anything that I thought would get other kids to accept me. If they were smoking, I'd smoke. If a boy wanted something sexual from me, I'd give in. When drugs were passed out, I'd try them.
>
> I tried to look beautiful. I tried to be popular. I tried for top grades, and dreamed of a high-status career. But by the time I got to college, I'd decided that I was a nobody, and life was a big hoax. Everybody was just going through the motions of living, pretending that what they thought and chose really mattered. You could only exist if you put on an act to other people as well as to yourself.[2]

thinking like a christian

Look again at all the ways that Kathy used to try to feel better about herself. List each activity under one of the following two headings:

the good   the bad

None of those things, even the "good" activities, brought Kathy the happiness and sense of self–worth she longed for. Why not?

_____

_____

Kathy was looking for love in all the wrong places. She was faking her inner feelings by projecting an outward character that was not true on the inside. She had neglected the spiritual dimension of her life.

neglecting the spirit

> Francis A. Schaeffer sums up: "The basic psychological problem is trying to be what we are not, and trying to carry what we cannot carry. Most of all, the basic problem is not being willing to be the creatures we are before the Creator" (UTT, 194).

What do you think Schaeffer meant by describing the basic problem as "not being willing to be the creatures we are before the Creator"?

_____

_____

the rest of the story

> A proper understanding of man's nature does not, however, end with affirming the existence of a spirit within man. The Christian position goes on to define man's nature as inherently evil because of man's decision to disobey God in the Garden of Eden. This understanding of man's sinful bent is critical for understanding man's nature and mental processes (UTT, 193-4).

According to the Christian view, what is the source of our psychological problems?

_____

If our sinful bent is the problem, what is the solution? _____

_____

_____

The key to helping people work through psychological problems is to help them recognize their responsibility for their own thoughts and actions.

biblical psychology to the rescue

The following passages describe the process of taking responsibility for your own thoughts and actions. After each set of verses, write out what action is needed to apply the passage to your life:

Romans 3:22-26 -

_____

_____

Colossians 1:13-14 -

_____

_____

John 1:12 -

_____

_____

the rest of kathy's story

As it turns out Kathy came to realize her spiritual condition and her need for God's forgiveness. "She bowed her head and said, 'Thank you, God. I accept your gift for me.' Kathy found a new self-knowledge and understanding of her personal worth after she chose to accept God's offer of total and complete forgiveness. Her "act" was over."[3]

Have you made the wonderful discovery of experiencing God's love and forgiveness? If not, talk with your pastor or Bible study leader about it this week.

If you have already accepted Jesus Christ as your Savior, then thank Him for giving you a new life, inner peace, and the pathway toward a meaningful life!

---

review key verse: **Colossians 2:13**

"When you were _____ in your sins and in the uncircumcision of your _____ nature, God made you alive with Christ. He forgave us all our sins . . . "

---

day 3 summary:

The first step to being a whole person is to admit you are sinful creature before a holy and loving God.

thinking like a christian

a child of the king

once upon a time . . .

. . . in a distant land, a son was born to the king and queen. But the baby boy was kidnapped and sold to a traveling merchant. A few years later the merchant and his wife died of a fever, leaving the young boy to fend for himself. The boy lived in poverty, begging food and sleeping in little shelters made from sticks.

On the twentieth anniversary of his son's birth, the king once again summoned his most trusted servant to go out in search of the prince. The servant had gone out many times before and had always come back with no news of the royal son. But at the king's bidding, he set out yet another time to find the son who would now have grown into a man.

At dusk on the third day, the servant stopped to rest his horse beside a clear-flowing stream when a young man came up to beg for bread. As the servant handed him a small loaf from his pack, he noticed an unusual mark on the young man's right hand. It was the birthmark of the prince!

The servant joyously told the beggar about his real identity and took him back to the castle to be united with his royal family. The prince lived happily ever after in the joy and bounty of the royal palace.

Like all fables, this make-believe story teaches us a principle about life. If the baby son represents a new-born Christian, what is the point of the story?

_____

_____

_____

the royal you

The story of the royal son illustrates an important biblical principle. The Bible describes Christians as ". . . a chosen people, a royal priesthood, a holy nation, a people belonging to God. . . ." **(1 Peter 2:9).**

Did you realize that as a Christian, you are a child of the King of Kings? But sometimes, like the son in the story, we are not aware of our royal spiritual heritage, and as a result, live in spiritual "poverty," not experiencing the really good stuff available to us by birthright.

Describe a Christian living in spiritual "poverty":

_____

_____

You do not need to live in spiritual poverty. Understanding your identity in Christ will propel you three giant steps forward to experiencing all the great things that God has in store for you.

week 5

You cannot experience the joys of the royal palace unless you know your royal status.

Find the following verses in your Bible and fill in the blanks to underscore the significant things that are true of you as a child of the King! (NOTE: This may seem like a lot of verses to look up, but the time you spend will be well worth the effort. So hang in there!)

John 1:12 - I am a _____ of God.

15:16 - I am chosen and appointed by Christ to bear His _____.

Romans 8:1 - I am free forever from _____.

8:17 - I am a joint _____ with Christ, sharing His inheritance with Him.

I Corinthians 6:17 - I am _____ with the Lord and am one spirit with Him.

6:19, 20 - I have been _____ with a price; I am not my own; I belong to God.

2 Corinthians 5:17 - I am a new_____.

5:21 - I have been made _____.

Galatians 2:20 - Christ lives in _____. The life I am now living is Christ's life.

Ephesians 1:3 - I have been blessed with every _____ blessing.

1:4 - I was chosen in Christ before the foundation of the world to be _____, and I am without blame before Him.

Colossians 2:7 - I am firmly _____ in Christ and am now being built up in Him.

2:10 - I have been made _____ in Christ.

2 Timothy 1:7 - I have been given a Spirit of _____, love, and self-discipline.

Hebrews 4:16 - I have the right to come boldly before the throne of God to receive _____ and find grace to help in time of need.

II Peter 1:4 - I have been given precious and magnificent promises by God, by which I am a partaker of God's _____ nature.

I John 5:18 - I am born of _____, and the evil one cannot touch me.

(The above study has been adapted from Neil T. Anderson's, *Victory Over the Darkness*, Regal Books, 1990).

meditating on God's view of you

Read out loud the above list every day for the next two weeks. Think about what it means to be a child of God. When you are tempted to sin, remember that you have God's mighty power working in you.

Use Paul's words to express a prayer to God for His ability to change you from the inside:

> **Now to him who is able to do immeasurably more than all we ask or imagine, according to his power that is at work within us, to him be glory in the church and in Christ Jesus throughout all generations, for ever and ever! Amen. (Ephesians 3:20-21)**

day 4 summary:

When you trust Jesus Christ as your Savior, you become a child of the King.

exploring the world of ideas:

If you have not checked out the papers this week for articles dealing with worldview topics, take a few minutes to do it now.

total commitment

the chicken, the cow and total commitment

A chicken and a cow were walking together when they passed a restaurant with a sign in the window which read, "Breakfast Special: Steak and eggs, $4.50." The chicken suggested that they both go in for a meal. The cow replied, "For you, that would be just a contribution. But for me, that means total commitment!"

O.K., so it's another semi-funny story. But, as usual, it has a point. If the chicken and cow represent two different attitudes towards being a Christian, how would you describe each one:

The chicken is like a person who . . . _____

_____

The cow represents someone who . . . _____

_____

You probably know some friends who are like the chicken in the above story– willing to make a "contribution" to the cause of Christ, spend a little time at church, basically be a "nice" person, don't murder anybody, stay out of trouble with the law, but the "total commitment" thing, you've got to be kidding!

living like a pig

Living on the fringe of the Christian life can also be compared to another farm animal, namely a pig! In *How to be your Own Selfish Pig*, Susan Schaeffer Macaulay tells you how you can become one by using the following **morning routine:**

"I gotta be me!"

Get up early enough to spend several hours on your personal appearance... look in the mirror and practice several key lines: "I gotta be me." "This doesn't meet my needs right now." "Hey, give me a little space!" "I can't help it; that's just the way I am." . . . As you walk [out the door], make a mental list of whom to say hello to and whom to ignore. . . . If you're ever at a loss for words to express your superiority over other human beings, simply apply the tip of your index finger to the tip of your nose and push upward gently.[4]

Of course, all people are free to live as selfish pigs if they choose. But the principles in the following verses should be a warning about the consequences of that type of self-centered pursuit. Read each passage and answer the questions:

Hebrews 10:26-31:

1) What indications in this passage tell you that this is written to Christians?

_____

_____

2) If a Christian keeps on sinning deliberately, what can he expect from God? _____

_____

3) What might some of those judgments be? _____

_____

4) Complete the verse: "It is a _____ thing to fall into the hands of the _____ God."

Proverbs 3:11-12:

1) As a child of God, you are called His _____.

2) The writer uses the analogy of a father and son. In what two ways does the father relate to his son?

_____

_____

3) Because a father loves his son, he _____ his son. God, as our heavenly father, loves us enough to discipline us when we live selfishly.
This should cause us to respond in what way?

(Check your answer)

☐ By being angry at God for His discipline and staying away from Him.

☐ By not "losing heart" and being encouraged that God cares.

☐ By having a "don't care" attitude and being discouraged.

"The question is, 'Who's the center of the universe, you or God?' "

pick your **barnyard personality**

Honestly, which barnyard animal are you more like in your Christian life?
(Circle your answer)

A) the chicken - willing to contribute a little
B) the pig - thinking mostly of yourself
C) the cow - totally committed to Jesus

If you circled "A" or "B," the more important question for you is: which one would you like to be? In light of the ultimate sacrifice that Jesus made for you, is there any good reason to live a "chicken" or "pig" type of Christian life? _____

positive **psychological health!**

Schaeffer outlines a simple approach to "positive psychological hygiene": "As a Christian, instead of putting myself in practice at the center of the universe, I must do something else. This is not only right, and the failure to do so is not only sin, but it is important for me personally in this life. I must think after God, and I must will after God" UTT, 198).

List some practical ways that you can think and will after God:

1) _____

2) _____

3) _____

day 5 summary:

Living a self-centered life invites God's discipline. Remaining in submission to Christ is the key to spiritual well-being and psychological health.

week 5 summary:

Biblical Christian psychology deals with tne total "you": body and soul. By trusting Jesus as your Savior, God accepts you as His child. Positive self esteem is a result of replacing your negative thoughts about yourself with God's perspective. By continuing to focus on God's view of you, you will be motivated to submit to the Lordship of Christ and live a life that is pleasing to Him.

---

review key verse: **Colossians 2:13**

"When you were dead in your sins and in the uncircumcision of your sinful nature, God made you _____ with Christ. He forgave us all our sins . . ."

ENDNOTES
[1] *How To Be Your Own Selfish Pig*, Susan Schaeffer Macaulay, (Zondervan Corporation, 1982) pp. 84-85.
[2] Ibid, p. 85.
[3] Ibid, p. 87.
[4] Ibid, pp. 106-107.

notes:

is there any real right or wrong?

Of course there is "right" and "wrong," you may be saying. You were probably brought up to know that certain things are right to do and other things are wrong. But have you ever stopped to think about where these ideas of "right and wrong" come from?

Some people believe that society decides what is acceptable behavior, with some cultures developing different moral standards from others. If this is true, then morality is what you have been raised to believe. But are those ideas true for someone living in a different culture half way around the globe? Or how about someone living five hundred years ago? Or five hundred years in the future? Maybe five hundred years from now they will have a different moral code.

And besides, who's to say what is the right thing to do, anyway? It all depends on the situation, right. . . or is that wrong?

This week, you will find out

> . . . "who says" what is right and what is wrong ◄ ∙∙∙∙∙∙∙∙∙∙∙∙∙∙∙∙∙∙∙∙∙∙∙∙∙∙∙∙∙∙∙∙∙∙

> . . . what's an "absolute" and how mankind has distorted God's moral standards

> . . . the greatest way you can please God and how to put that into your daily experience

> . . . if feeling "guilty" is good

> . . . how to maintain a close relationship with the God of the Universe!

week 6

---

key verse for week 6: **Colossians 3:17**
"And whatever you do, whether in word or deed, do it all in the name of the Lord Jesus, giving thanks to God the Father through him."

the grand "says who?"

first, a little test

Circle the word that you feel best completes the sentence according to your ethical worldview:

"I play the game of

life by my own rules!"

- Drinking and driving is (**irresponsible/responsible**)?
- Pushing a little child down a staircase is (**perverse/life-enhancing**)?
- Taking your share of the chores is (**evil/good**)?
- Poking a sharp stick in another person's eye is (**revolting/entertaining**)?

Why did you circle those words? _____

_____

It may seem obvious that some behavior is right and other actions are wrong. It just makes common sense to not drink and drive, and it seems revolting to poke a stick in someone's eye. But why are these things wrong? Where do these ideas of "right and wrong" come from?

Where did you get your ideas about ethics? _____

But there is something you have to consider: **in our society there are many conflicting views about what is right or wrong.** When different sources give conflicting moral values, how do you decide which one to follow? Or, in other words,

"Who says" this is right and that is wrong?

Good questions! Let's consider some answers.

the idea of **moral law**

Christian writer and philosopher C. S. Lewis said it this way:

> Think of a country where people were admired for running away from battle, or where a man felt proud of double-crossing all the people who had been kindest to him. You might just as well try to imagine a country where two and two make five. . . . Men have differed as to whether you should have one wife or four. But they have always agreed that you must not simply have any woman you liked.[1]

English sociologist David Martin has cited the International Values Survey to conclude that . . .

> . . . we are mostly agreed about good and bad. People are, it seems, adamantly opposed to lying, stealing, cheating, coveting, killing, and dishonoring their parents.[2]

Based on these two quotes, what can you conclude concerning the origin of ethics?

_____

_____

ethics and theology

"We are mostly agreed about good and bad."

> Christian ethics is inseparable from theology because Christian ethics is grounded in the character of God. "One of the distinctions of the Judeo-Christian God," says Francis Schaeffer, "is that not all things are the same to Him. That at first may sound rather trivial, but in reality it is one of the most profound things one can say about the Judeo Christian God. He exists; He has a character; and not all things are the same to Him. Some things conform to His character, and some are opposed to His character." The task of Christian ethics is determining what conforms to God's character and what does not (UTT, p. 115).

According to Schaeffer, what is one of the most profound things about Biblical Christianity? _____

_____

A unique aspect of a biblical worldview is that ethics is tied into the _____ of God. So to the question, "Who says what is right and wrong?", the answer is,

"God says, that's who!"

Therefore, ethics have a source, or origin, that flows directly from God's character. If this is so, then what should we do to determine what is right and wrong?

_____

_____

"But Skip, that assumes you know EVERYTHING about the game."

God's character: basis for ethics

Which of the three characteristics of God noted in week 2, day 3 relates most closely to our discussion of "ethics"? _____

How does God's "righteousness" provide a foundation for ethics? _____

_____

God's character and you

Spend a few minutes reflecting on the holiness of God. Read Psalm 96:9-13. Based on this psalm, write your thoughts concerning God's holiness and your behavior.

_____

_____

day 1 summary:

Ethics are grounded in the character of God.

moral absolutes? absolutely!
it all depends!

You've probably heard it said . . .

"Who's to say what's right? What's right for you might not be right for someone else. Everything depends on the situation."

What do you think of that statement? Write a short critique:

_____

_____

If everything is "relative", that would mean there are no "absolute" standards of right and wrong. However, the Biblical Christian worldview claims to give a moral "standard" to gauge what is right. See if you can follow the logic of this next statement as you fill in the appropriate worldview categories:
(Theology, Philosophy, Biology, Psychology, Ethics)

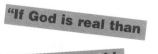
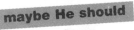

if . . . God is real (as we learned in our study of P_____),
and God's character is righteous (from our study of T_____),
and God designed life to work in a certain way (our study of B_____),
and God made man to reflect His character (from biblical P_____),

then . . . it follows that there are absolute standards of conduct that are
true for all people, in all situations, and throughout all time, (as we are
discovering in our current study of E_____).

Do you see the connection between all the worldview categories that we have studied so far?

what's an "absolute"?

When we talk about an "absolute" standard, it refers to a standard that does not change. Think about a ruler or tape measure; an inch is the same no matter where you live or in what circumstances you may find yourself.

In the same way, God has established absolute moral standards that do not change with location, situation, or culture.   A **moral absolute** is true for all _____, at all _____, and in ____ situations.

Biblical Christianity emphatically embraces the concept of moral absolutes. But what specific absolutes make up the moral order? Write a short list:

wow!

A moral absolute is true for all people, at all times, in all situations.

_____   _____

_____   _____

_____   _____

the absolute nature of ethical absolutes

> Absolutes are revealed to man in the Bible. While it is impossible for every situation requiring moral decisions to be contained in the Bible, the Christian is given enough specific values and guidelines to have a sense of what is right and what is wrong in all situations. The most obvious absolutes, of course, are the Ten Commandments–the Decalogue. This acts as the "basic law" for mankind, but it is not the only law revealed in the Bible. Much of the Old Testament is dedicated to describing God's moral order. (UTT, 119)

check it out!

God's commands and general principles form a "moral framework" for making ethical decisions.

The Bible is not one long list of "do's and dont's" that cover every aspect of your life. God created you as a free moral agent. You have the ability to make moral choices. This means that, in the Scriptures, God's commands and His general principles form a "moral _____" from which we all make ethical decisions.

"ideas have consequences."

Each of the following passages describes the way that God designed human relationships to work best. In the chart below, summarize God's moral plan, then write the ways that people have distorted it due to their sin, and in the last column list some of the consequences of trying to live outside of God's moral framework.

	God's moral plan	Man's distortion	Negative Consequences
Genesis 2:22-24 -			
Proverbs 12:22 -			
Matthew 6:25-27 -			
1 Corinthians 6:18-20 -			

If we follow man's distorted ideas about God's moral design, there are significant and negative consequences to those actions.

On the other hand, what would the world be like if everyone, in every place, would always practice the following general principles:

	God's moral plan	Positive consequences
Genesis 2:22-24 -	A family consists of a man and a woman loving each other for life.	
Proverbs 12:22 -	Tell the truth.	
Matthew 6:25-27 -	Trust God for the future.	
1 Corinthians 6:18-20 -	Reserve sexual intimacy for marriage.	

thinking like a christian

morality in the "real" world

Look for examples of how "ideas have consequences." Check the newspaper or a weekly news magazine for articles to illustrate people's moral choices. Bring these to your next group session to discuss with your friends.

day 2 summary:

> Because God is real, holy and wise, there are moral absolutes that govern the way we live.

the greatest

If you had to pick just one ethical law as the most important to follow, what would you choose?

The greatest ethical law is: _____

_____

Jesus had some things to say about the greatest of God's standards. Read **Mark 12:28-31,** and write in your own words the most important ethical principle according to Jesus: _____

_____

What does it mean to love God with all your heart?

_____

. . .with all your soul?

_____

. . .with all your mind?

_____

. . .with all your strength?

_____

wow!

Loving God is more than just an emotion.

if you want to be **happy** . . .

"The moral end, or highest good, is the glory of God," writes William Young. "In declaring by word and deed the perfections, especially the moral perfections of the most High, man finds true happiness" (UTT, 120).

The above quote mentions how to find true happiness.

What is it? _____

Can you list some of "God's perfections"? _____

_____

William Young suggests that we achieve true happiness as we seek to express the moral attributes of God.

How could you "declare by word" the perfections of God? _____

_____

In what ways could you "declare by deed" the perfections of God? _____

_____

_____

loving God by loving others

Jesus' words in Mark 12 point to a **second** commandment. The idea is that our love for God will overflow into our love for our fellow man. If we truly love God, one way we can demonstrate that love is through _____ our fellow man.

check it out!

> The love of God is the service of man in love (UTT, 120).

meeting real needs

> This duty toward our fellow man requires more than serving his spiritual needs. "[M]an is more than a soul destined for another world;" says Norman Geisler, "he is also a body living in this world. And as a resident of this time-space continuum man has physical and social needs which cannot be isolated from spiritual needs. Hence, in order to love man as he is–the whole man–one must exercise a concern about his social needs as well as his spiritual needs" (UTT, 120).

According to Jesus' story about the good Samaritan in **Luke 10:29-37**, a "neighbor" is defined as anyone you know who has a need.

Does someone you know qualify as your "neighbor"? _____

Who would that be, and what is their physical need? _____

_____

Specifically, how can you demonstrate God's love by helping to meet that physical need? _____

_____

_____

putting love into practice

Why not put into practice what you are learning about loving God and loving others? You may want to sing a praise chorus that describes the majesty of God. Singing reminds you about the moral character of God and helps to imprint those thoughts in your mind.

Then, in quiet reflection, ask God how you can "declare His perfections" in deed. As He brings people and thoughts to your mind, write down specific ways that you can demonstrate love toward a "neighbor."

1) _____

2) _____

3) _____

wow!

Inspiration without perspiration leads to frustration.

day 3 summary:

Loving God involves your heart, soul, mind and strength and serving others.

review key verse: **Colossians 3:17**
"And whatever you do, whether in _____ or _____, do it all in the name of the Lord Jesus, giving thanks to God the Father through him."

the ultimate guilt trip
the moral ozone hole!

"Our Nation is

experiencing

a moral ozone hole."

In today's society, it's becoming increasingly difficult to follow God's ethical standards. Our whole culture is moving quickly away from a moral perspective to one of "doing your own thing." It's as if we are living in a

. . . "moral" ozone hole

According to a survey of nearly 7,000 high school and college students taken a few years ago. . .

. . . one third of the high school students said that they had taken an item from a store without paying for it within the previous year.

. . . 60% had lied to their parents.

. . . honesty ranked lower in their priorities than getting into college and securing a well-paying job.[3]

Lying, stealing, dishonesty. These deal with some pretty basic moral ideas. As this kind of behavior becomes more wide-spread, what would you expect will happen to our society? _____

_____

everyone behaving badly

Maybe someone should produce a movie called *Everyone Behaving Badly*. Have you noticed anyone behaving badly in your community? In what ways?

Make a short list:

1)   4)

2)   5)

3)   6)

Why do you think people act this way? _____

_____

Read **Romans 1:16-20** for a good answer to the above question. It seems that people everywhere are aware of God's moral laws, but they refuse to obey them. Why? _____

_____

_____

Have you ever tried to talk to non-Christians about their basic sin nature? Try bringing up the word "sin" in a conversation with your friends and see what happens! You'll probably hear:

> "Don't start preaching to me about what's right and wrong! You can't put that guilt trip on me."

How would you respond to that kind of comment? _____

_____

the "guilt" alarm

To help you get a handle on "guilt," think about an alarm clock. What's the purpose of an alarm clock? It alerts you when it's time to wake up. You may not like the alarm clock waking you from a sound sleep, but you don't blame it for doing what it is supposed to do!

check it out!

> Social disintegration is the result of moral disintegration.

Guilt is a moral alarm clock.

83

Guilt is like an alarm clock. Feelings of guilt are a "wake up" call to alert you to your need to turn from that sinful behavior and ask for God's forgiveness.

> This conviction of guilt is crucial for a Christian to understand the incredible sacrifice God made when He sent His Son to die for us. The Christian ethical code calls for perfection, and no man other than Christ has ever achieved that. Thus, it is the ethical code itself that points man first to his own sinful nature and then to the realization that the only One who can save him is the Man who has not stepped outside the moral code, Jesus Christ. The absolute moral code shows us our absolute dependence on Him (UTT, 121).

Why should you talk to your friends about God's moral standards? _____

_____

The next time you are talking with your non-Christian friends, don't be afraid to talk about "sin." Of course, you shouldn't use it as a club to beat them over the head but gently as a way to introduce them to the real world.

making it happen where you live

When Jesus stepped out of eternity into time, He provided the solution to our sin problem. Read **Revelation 22:16-17,** and write these verses in your own words:

_____

_____

_____

Pray for your friends who need to understand their sin problem AND the solution to their sin problem found in Jesus Christ. How can you, in a tactful way, help them understand the real reason that people behave badly?

_____

_____

day 4 summary:

Feelings of guilt are good when they lead us to seek God's love and forgiveness.

have you . . . checked your local newspaper and cut out an article or two that describe the moral "ozone hole" we are living in? Be ready to discuss them from a biblical worldview when you bring them to the next group session.

personal moral inventory

just don't talk about . . .

Look up **Revelation 21:8**. What is the destination for people who disobey God's moral law?_____

A fiery lake of burning sulfur is not a very encouraging picture. From this passage and others, the Bible speaks of a time in the future when God will judge non-Christians for their conduct.

But someone might say, "Don't talk about that 'fire and brimstone' stuff. What are you trying to do, scare people into accepting Christ?"

Well, what's your opinion? Should you tell people about...you know...the other place...(HELL)? What do you think?

- ☐ Yes, tell them about "Hell"
- ☐ No, fear is not a good motivator
- ☐ I'm not sure, convince me!

motivated by . . . "fear"?

Is "fear" a good motivator? To answer that question, think about this: **Why do you warn your little sister not to play in the street or touch a hot stove?**

_____

_____

Of course, people can be motivated by either fear or love. That's why the "gospel" is like the two sides of a coin. When we are sharing the "good news," we obviously are referring to God's love and forgiveness. But unless people also understand that God will judge sin (which is "bad news"), they may not be motivated to respond to God's love.

We shouldn't dismiss either side of the gospel "coin" as we try to help our friends understand their need to accept Christ as Savior and Lord.

Paul said the same thing in **II Corinthians 5:10-11** . . .

> **For we must all appear before the judgment seat of Christ. Since, then, we know what it is to fear the Lord, we try to persuade men.**

Fear is a
great motivator.

what's the connection?

What does all this talk about sin and punishment have to do with our study of Ethics? Plenty! First of all, it points out the fact that God takes sin seriously. And if He takes the sins of non-Christians seriously, He also takes the sins of Christians seriously.

Turn to **2 Peter 3:9-14**. Read the entire passage. The subject concerns God's future judgment of the entire earth. In light of God's judgment, how should you be living today? _____

_____

> The Christian cannot, however, simply rely on Christ to save him, and then continue in his sinful ways. Rather, once the Christian understands the ultimate sacrifice God made for him, he cannot help but respond with a grateful desire to please God by adhering to His moral order (UTT, 121).

Once you see the magnitude of your sin problem, it causes you to see the magnitude of God's love. Jesus said the same thing in **Luke 7:36-50**. What is the point that Jesus is making in this passage? _____

_____

staying in a right relationship with God

Even though you may have become His child by receiving Jesus as your Savior, you still at times disobey His moral commands. This disobedience is taken seriously by God and breaks your fellowship with Him.

There is a way to restore fellowship with God once we realize we have sinned. The process is based on a verse in the book of 1 John.

Look up **1 John 1:9** and fill in the blanks below:

> If we _____ our sins, he is _____ and just and will
> _____ us our sins and purify us from all unrighteousness.

This verse offers some principles that allow you to maintain a close walk with God.

"abc's" of walking with God

The "A" stands for **"Agree"** with God concerning your sin. Don't try to make excuses for what you have done. God wants you to simply admit that you were wrong-- that's what "confession" means.

Are you aware of any areas in your life that you need to confess to God? If so, do it now.

week 6

The "B" stands for **"Believe"** God's promise. In **1 John 1:9** He states that He will cleanse you of your unrighteous behavior. Did you notice that God's forgiveness is based on His character? What two aspects of God's character form the basis for His forgiveness?

1) _____

2) _____

God is right to forgive you because Jesus paid the penalty for your sin. God took the punishment that you deserve and placed it on Jesus when He died on the cross. In that way, God's justice has been met.

> **If you confessed your sin(s) to God, do you now believe that He has forgiven you of all your sins?**

_____

> **If so, thank Him for His unconditional love and forgiveness to experience His complete cleansing.**

_____

_____

"Being filled with the Holy Spirit is the only way to go!"

week 6

The "C" stands for **"control."** This means that you want to allow Jesus Christ to direct your life – every part of it. Look up **Ephesians 5:18**. This verse says that you should **not** do something and that you should do something.

What should you **not** do? _____

What should you do? _____

Being "filled" with the Spirit simply means allowing the Holy Spirit to influence and control your life. Write a prayer that focuses on your desire to allow Christ's Spirit to fill you in each area of your life.

_____

_____

_____

_____

day 5 summary:

God judges Christians for how they live morally. Confessing our sin puts us back into a right relationship with God.

week 6 summary:

Our culture today is screaming that morality doesn't matter. Yet, all of human history declares two important truths:

> #1 - everybody understands there are certain moral standards, and
>
> #2 - everybody breaks those standards.

That is why only the Biblical Christian worldview makes any sense. Because there is a God who is holy and righteous, then each person can seek God's forgiveness for disobeying His moral code. Only then can man experience true inner peace and begin the journey into living for God according to His moral law.

---

review key verse: **Colossians 3:17**

"And whatever you do, whether in word or deed, do it all in the name of the Lord Jesus, _____ _____ to God the Father through him."

ENDNOTES

[1] Quoted in *Not So Christian America*, Thomas C. Reeves, *First Things*, October 1996, p.18.

[2] Ibid.

[3] *Honesty May No Longer be the Best Policy*, Richard Morin, *Washington Post Weekly*, Dec. 7, 1997, p.36.

notes:

sociology

what makes a healthy society?

Have you ever noticed how few hermits there are in the world? Most folks just naturally want to be around other people.

"Sociology" deals with this issue of living together. As a part of an overall worldview, it asks the question: "What is the basis for a healthy society?" According to the Bible, there are at least three ways people live together; the family, the church, and the state.

Living in a healthy society sounds good, but we quickly realize that each level of society has its own benefits and pitfalls. The family can be a place of great love and blessing or one of fear and abuse. Churches can fulfill their role of spreading the "gospel" and serving those in need or fall apart into factions. The state can be a source of unifying people to protect God-given rights of life and liberty, or it can become a bureaucracy which imposes high taxes and takes away freedom from the people.

This week you will explore God's design for society. You will discover that His plan for the family and the church provides the very best way to develop as individuals and to get along with other people. The institution of the state will be discussed more fully under the topic of "politics" in a couple of weeks.

This week, you can expect to learn about . . .

- what it means to be a "social" creature
- the vital signs of a healthy society ◄
- how to change our society for the better
- why families are the bedrock of all societies
- the importance of the church for maintaining a civilized culture!

So share with your family the things that you are learning this week. You'll be glad you did, and so will they!

"Chris," says Skip, "If the following statement applied to you, how would you fill in the blank?"

"i am a _____ animal."

Chris thought a minute and said, "Party, as in "party animal!"
"I don't think so." replied Skip. "That may describe me but definitely not you. Try again."

"O.K. Skip, how about 'intelligent'?"

"Definitely a strong maybe. But even though you are in the top ten percent of our class, you're a little slim on "common sense," came the rebuttal from Skip. "I know, you are a featherless bi-pedal animal! But then again, so is a plucked chicken!"

Skip laughed and crowed as he walked away, leaving Chris wondering why he brought up the subject in the first place.

Well, what are some other possible answers to the statement? Chris might have said he was a **social** animal. What do you think about that answer? Does it fit you, too?

If we are serious, we all would admit that deep down, we are social creatures. Do you know why? Complete this sentence:
We are social creatures because _____

back to the past

It seems that we can't get away from going back to our biblical theology to answer questions that come from other categories, like this question that deals with sociology. Open your Bible to **Genesis 1- 2,** and answer with the following questions:

In chapter one, we are told that God liked all that He created. Scan the chapter for the phrase that describes His creation: (see verses 10, 12,18, 21, 25, 31)

"God saw that it was _____."

In Genesis 2 we are introduced to some details that are not included in the overview of creation in Chapter 1. What is one of the first things God said after creating Adam? (See 2:18)

"It is _____ good for the man to be _____."

week 7

God knew something about the man He had just created; Adam was not made to be alone. After stating that there was no helper suitable for Adam, God created _____ (Read 2:19-20). Do you find it interesting that God brought all those animals to Adam? Why do you think He did that?

_____

In naming the animals, apparently God was giving Adam an object lesson from nature. As Adam studied and named all the animals, he must have recognized that there were male and female counterparts. Yet, as he looked around, he began to realize that there was no counterpart for him! No suitable helper was found.

Adam must have experienced loneliness.

You know what happens next. Review **Genesis 2:21-23,** and notice Adam's comment when he first saw Eve. Our English translation doesn't convey the original language as well, but Adam's response was more of a . . .

"wow, finally someone like me!"

Was he excited, or what? If you had been Adam, you would have been excited, too.

Finally, the writer gives us a general principle based on the account of Adam and Eve. Look at verse 24.

"For this reason a man will _____ his father and mother and be _____ to his wife, and they will become ___ flesh."

S.D. Gaede stresses the inherent social nature of man, stating, "God designed the human being to be a relational creature. Note this point well. Humankind was created to relate to other beings. It was not an accident. It was not the result of sin. It was an intentional, creational given" (UTT, 228).

Relating to other people is a part of our inherent nature. It is God's design. We are designed to be _____.

check it out!

Man was created as a social being.

week 7

God meets our social needs

When Adam saw Eve, he recognized God's provision for his social needs. How is God providing for your social needs? _____

_____

Write a prayer of thanksgiving to God for the special people He has brought within your social circle. _____

_____

91

> **week 7 key verse: Colossians 3:15**
> "Let the peace of Christ rule in your hearts, since as members of one body you were called to peace. And be thankful."

day 1 summary:

God created us as social beings.

week 7 day 2

what's wrong with society?

society's vital signs

A medical doctor checks certain "vital signs" to determine a patient's health. This might include checking the pulse, heart-beat, and breathing. If these are within a certain range, the patient is healthy. But if one or more are outside normal limits, the patient has cause for concern.

Like an individual, a society has certain "vital signs" that indicate the condition of that culture. What might be some of those signs? Write as many as you can: (the first is done for you)

Crime rate _____   _____

_____   _____

_____   _____

"Our culture is showing
some very disturbing
signs of ill-health."

Below is a list of vital cultural areas. Circle one of the numbers on the scale after each area to indicate how you feel our culture is doing here in the United States:

	healthy				sick
crime rate	1	2	3	4	5
divorce rate	1	2	3	4	5
stable families	1	2	3	4	5
physical abuse	1	2	3	4	5
drug/alcohol abuse	1	2	3	4	5
sexual conduct	1	2	3	4	5
education	1	2	3	4	5
politics	1	2	3	4	5
voter turnout	1	2	3	4	5
volunteer organizations	1	2	3	4	5

So, how do you feel our society is doing? Is it healthy or hurting?
What was the average score that you gave our society? _____

diagnosing the problem

So what's the problem? Why is our society unhealthy? Let's go back to the medical analogy. When a patient has a fever, the doctor does not treat the fever. Do you know why? _____

_____

The fever is not the problem. The fever is just a symptom of the real problem, which might be a virus in the body. The doctor treats the virus, not the fever. When the virus is eliminated, then the fever goes away.

In the same way, the disturbing social trends around us are only symptoms of an underlying problem. That brings us back to the question: What's the problem with society? Take a guess: _____

> "If man's behavior were somehow conditioned by genetic code or social externals," says William Stanmeyer, "then no just judge could blame him for the evil he commits. But the scripture teaches unequivocally that God blamed Adam and Eve for succumbing to the temptation to disobedience and punished them accordingly" (UTT, 226).

There are basically three options as to the source of our social problems. Put a check by the source that is based on a biblical worldview :

- ☐ Genetic makeup
- ☐ External social pressure
- ☐ Individual sinful choices

> The Christian view grants individual man much more control over his society, but it also burdens him with much more responsibility. Man, in the Christian perspective, must face the consequences of his decisions. This point is made painfully clear in the opening chapters of Genesis, when Adam and Eve bring a curse on the whole human race and are exiled from the Garden of Eden, all because they choose to disobey God (UTT, 226).

Re-read that text box again and think about the implications of just two people's disobedience to God.

Disobeying God's moral principles brings negative consequences on not only the individual who breaks the moral code but also has a ripple effect throughout society. Like a rock thrown into a pond, the ripples eventually reach the entire surface of the pond.

nypd blue . . . for real!

Let's say that a local grocery store is robbed. Trace the ripple effect that takes place throughout the community when one person acts outside of God's moral law. What might be the consequences for each of the following people in the community:

the robber: _____

the police officer: _____

the grocer: _____

the average shopper: _____

local tax payers: _____

Don't treat the symptom, treat the problem.

a spiritual cure

Most social problems originate from individual problems. Therefore, when we talk about the many negative social trends we see today, we must face the fact that the solution is a moral and spiritual one for the individuals who make up that society.

A biblical worldview points to the cure for the problem of sin.
Read **2 Corinthians 5:17**. Write the verse in your own words:

_____

_____

_____

The possibility for change is real. And when enough individuals change for the better, you will have a healthy society.

Write a prayer expressing your desire to be a part of the **solution** in building a healthy society.

_____

_____

_____

day 2 summary:

Our society shows definite signs of being unhealthy.

how to change society
a "barn raising" experience

If you were going to build a two-story barn to store your hay and shelter your three cows and four horses (assuming, of course, that you actually own three cows and four horses). . .how long would you guess that it would take you to build an 8,000 square foot barn all by yourself?

week 7

☐ Two weeks
☐ Two months
☐ Two years
☐ Too much for one person to do!

If you guessed "Too much...", you're right on the money. One person could not easily build a building that large.

Remember back in the "old" days; how did the folks on the farm build a barn? They would call on all of their neighbors and have themselves a good ol' fashioned "barn raising." What one person could not do by himself, the community of people could accomplish as a group.

As we've seen the last couple of days, social problems are in reality a result of individual problems. Because the larger society is affected, it takes a community "barn raising" effort to see social change.

But in a "barn raising," everyone has a part. So now we have come full circle to the individual as the solution. If it's individuals who are the problem in society, then it takes individuals to solve the problem.

christianity **to the rescue**

Recall the story in the Bible of the Good Samaritan? Jesus told that story to show how we need to be involved in meeting the needs of a hurting neighbor. Christians throughout the ages have taken Christ's teaching to heart and sought out ways to help their neighbors and their whole society. Let's take a brief survey from the beginning of the Christian church to see how this has taken place.

hope **for civilization**

When the church was born, Roman civilization had brought peace and harmony to a large portion of the world. But within 400 years Roman culture fell to the sword of northern barbarians. During the next few centuries, chaos ruled Europe as warring bands of illiterate Germanic tribes opposed and deposed one another. Cities and cultural centers disappeared. Literacy, law, and order crumbled.

But one force prevented barbarism from completely taking over. What was that force? _____

It was the church! The medieval church modeled a counter-culture that kept the spark of civilization alive. Monks preserved not only the Scriptures but classical literature as well. They cleared land, built towns and harvested crops.

During the seventh century in France, the clergy were the best educated and least immoral group in Europe. The French monks ran schools, and sheltered orphans,

widows, paupers and slaves. They constructed aqueducts, opened hospitals and were respected by a population staggering under the greed and dishonesty of their political leaders. The same was true in Ireland, England, and other countries of western Europe.[1]

Because Christians got involved in society, the barbarous Dark Ages gave way to the light of Christian culture, and civilization was renewed.

hope for holland

What is true in the general sweep of history is equally true in the life of individual Christians who have sought to make a difference. An example can be seen in the life of **Abraham Kuyper**, a Dutch theologian and pastor in the early 1900's.

Kuyper worked diligently to influence public life in the Netherlands by founding a Christian university, publishing a newspaper, and even being elected prime minister. The social and educational reforms Kuyper initiated continue to benefit Holland today.[2]

Connect each area of society that Kuyper influenced with its corresponding world-view category:

a university	**The Media**
news reporting	**Government**
prime minister	**Sociology**
social reforms	**Education**

Why do you think Kuyper worked so diligently to influence these various social areas?

_____

What was it about Kuyper's worldview that lead him to social action?

_____

To Kuyper, there were not two realms to reality; the secular and the sacred. If God created the world and people and societies, then everything in the world of people and societies relates to Him. Therefore, Kuyper became involved in helping society in specific ways.

changed people change the world

There is a connection between our biblical view of life and our view of society. Christianity is not just a vertical relationship with God; it also involves a horizontal relationship with other people. This has been true throughout the history of the Christian church.

In what ways can you influence your social world? Make a short list, and then ask God to direct your steps in how you can be involved in a Christian "barn raising"!

1. _____

_____

2. _____

_____

3. _____

_____

day 3 summary:

> **Throughout history the church has been involved in transforming society by meeting social needs.**

review key verse: **Colossians 3:15**
"Let the peace of Christ rule in your hearts, since as members of one body you were called to _____. And be thankful."

why did God make **families?**

The Bible makes it clear that families are a part of God's plan for mankind. But why did He plan it that way? What's so important about families? Can you come up with three practical reasons?

1) _____
2) _____
3) _____

> For the Christian, marriage and the family are ordained by God (Genesis 2:23-25) and will always be the fundamental institution of society. The Christian believes that the family and its role are strictly defined in the Bible... (UTT, 229).

The family has been called the "first school of human _____." It has the ability to pass on traditions, history and discipline to provide a context for understanding the world.

Turn to **Deuteronomy 6:6-9,** and list the different ways that parents are to instruct their children:

1) _____   5) _____

2) _____   6) _____

3) _____   7) _____

4) _____   8) _____

Now, an even more important question is: why are parents to train their children by all of these methods? See **Deuteronomy 6:1-2**:

_____

It's been said that "repetition aids learning." If eight times a day you were hearing how God loves you and relates to everything you do, it would begin to sink in after a while!

what's a kid to do?

If parents are to do the teaching, then it just makes sense that children are to do the learning and obeying. Turn to **Exodus 20:12,** and read the fifth commandment (of the original ten!). What does God promise to children who honor their parents?

_____

Is this promise true? Check it out for yourself. Would a child lead a healthier and happier life if he obeyed the following instructions? If so, check the box:

parent's instruction	healthier/happier life?
Don't play in traffic	☐
Eat your spinach	☐
Share your toys with your sister	☐
Drive safely	☐
Don't take illegal drugs	☐
Save sexual intimacy for marriage	☐

You may not like it at the time, but eating your spinach gives you a healthier body. And when you are healthier, you are happier. You can see that it really does make a difference if you obey your parent's instructions.

check it out!

> The first school of human instruction is the family!

thinking like a christian

families **are important**

Do families have an influence on society? Consider Jonathan Edwards–pastor, scholar, and leader of the First Great Awakening (a time of spiritual renewal in America in the 1700's). He and his wife Sarah left a remarkable legacy to American society. They raised 11 children, and by 1900, the family had 1,400 descendants, including:

> **13** college presidents
> **65** professors
> **100** lawyers
> **30** judges
> **66** physicians
> **3** governors
> **3** senators
> and a vice president of the United States![4]

This is what can happen when parents give moral and spiritual instruction, and children do the obeying–a healthy family tradition is passed down from generation to generation, and society benefits.

family **first**

> It is to society's advantage to build and encourage the God-ordained social institution of marriage and the family (UTT, 229).

Studies agree with the biblical view of the family: marriage and families are important!

> After surveying more than 130 empirical studies, Professor Robert H. Coombs of the UCLA School of Medicine concluded: **"Married people live longer and generally are more emotionally and physically healthy than the unmarried."**[5]

Married people
live longer!

personal **reflection**

A saying goes: "If you want to marry a princess, you must first be a prince!" (Of course, the same holds true for you aspiring princesses out there.) What can you be doing now to develop into a prince or princess?

_____

_____

_____

day 4 summary:

God designed the family as the first place for moral instruction.

but is church good for me?
crime, health and happiness

One historian researched church attendance in England over the years. During the times that more people attended Sunday School, what do you think happened?

☐ fewer people attended soccer games
☐ the crime rate went down
☐ the farmers grew more crops
☐ more people got married

Do you know what this researcher found? When Sunday school attendance was highest, the crime rate was lowest. And conversely, when church attendance was low, crime rose!

Going to church does make a difference! Not only does history bear this out, but recent surveys tell the same story.

survey results: Dr. Dale Matthews of Georgetown University reviewed 212 studies and found that three-fourths showed a positive effect of religious commitment on a person's health. The research shows that people who attend church are both physically healthier and less depressed.[6]

You realize, of course, that just going and sitting in a pew is not what we are talking about. The key to success is believing and living biblical principles, not just warming a pew on Sunday mornings.

If you were to write a prescription for a happy, productive and healthy life based on the above statistics, what would it be?

_____

_____

the soul of society

> The church also can cause a society to face God by providing an example of true community. If the Christian church could show the rest of society that it is possible to live according to the command "Love your neighbor as yourself," then individuals and society might be more willing to turn to God and acknowledge Him as the initiator of all relations (UTT, 230).

Think about that paragraph. What will cause some people to turn to God?

_____

_____

this little light of mine

What happens when Christians retreat from being involved in society? Darkness. If we retreat from any area of our culture, the light flickers and goes out. All that is left is the darkness of man's ideas.

But Jesus has called us to be involved in spreading His light of righteousness. The reason that we go to church and learn more about a relationship with God is so we can be equipped to proclaim His love to others who are still in darkness. Read 1 Peter 2:9 below:

> **But you are a chosen people, a royal priesthood, a holy nation, a people belonging to God, that you may declare the praises of him who called you out of darkness into his wonderful light.**

As a member of the church, how can you challenge the culture this week, in school, with your friends, in your city? Really think about it, and list some ways:

1. _____
2. _____
3. _____

Review each summary statement from this week, and select three key areas to pray about:

key concept:		my prayer:
1) _____	:	_____
		_____
2) _____	:	_____
		_____
3) _____	:	_____

check it out!

Jesus said . . .
"You are the light of the world. A city on a hill cannot be hidden."
(Matthew 5:14)

week 7

day 5 summary:

The church must challenge individuals and society to live by God's moral standards.

 **summary:**

Biblical sociology focuses on three levels of society: the family, the church, and the state. All three, working together under God's direction, are needed for a healthy and happy society. Each level has its own purpose.

- The family is responsible for raising children and modeling Godly living.

- The church is called to meet the larger needs of society in the areas of evangelism, education and social action.

- The state is designed to maintain order and administer justice in society.

---

review key verse: **Colossians 3:15**

"Let the peace of Christ rule in your hearts, since as members of _____ _____ you were called to peace. And be thankful."

ENDNOTES

[1] *Against the Night*, Charles Colson, Servant Books, Ann Arbor, MI, 1989, p.133-4.

[2] *A Dance with Deception*, Charles Colson, Word, Dallas, TX, 1993, p.21.

[3] *Against the Night*, Charles Colson, Servant Books, Ann Arbor, MI, 1989, p.130.

[4] *Breakpoint* with Chuck Colson, January 1997, p.18.

[5] *The Family in America,* Focus on the Family, June 1991, p. 2-3.

[6] *Several Studies Link Good Health With Religious Belief, Prayer,* AP Wire Service, Statesville Record & Landmark, Tuesday, February 13, 1996, p. 8-A.

notes:

week 7

why so many laws?

Laws, laws everywhere and no place to hide! Everywhere you go there are laws.
Driving down the highway requires obeying traffic laws. When you make money,
there are laws for giving a percentage in taxes. As a teenager, there are certain rules
to follow about how late you can stay out or how long you can be on the phone.
Your friends expect you to be truthful (that's a rule that everyone expects you to follow; if you don't think so, just try *not* telling someone the truth and having them find
out!). In science, there are laws of chemistry and physics. Even in church there are
certain rules for worshiping God (for example: we do not offer blood sacrifices on an
altar; we do confess our sins to God).

We are surrounded by laws! When you think of "laws," do you have positive or
negative thoughts? Most would say "negative!" But guess what, laws don't have to
be so bad. Why not?

It's simple, really. It starts way back in our first week when we learned about the
nature of God. God is Relational, yes. He is Righteous, certainly. But He is also
RULER. God rules, and He designed the whole universe to work in synch with His
character.

So everything is designed to operate according to the laws God established–laws of
physics, laws of chemistry, laws of ethics, laws of civil government, laws of how to
worship Him–it's all a package deal. We live in a world of laws. That's the way
God designed it–and don't forget, God said that His design is "gooooood"! (See
Genesis 1:31)

This week you will

> . . . uncover the significance of the world of laws ◄
> . . . discern why we have laws and why laws are "good" to have
> . . . define what is meant by the term "natural law"
> . . . learn about biblical principles that rule our lives
> . . . explore the idea of "legislating morality"

Sound good? Good! Just remember, you WILL enjoy yourself while engaged in
these studies, and that's an order! (Ooooops, there's another "law.") Oh, well, it
seems you just can't escape them! So you might as well read on to understand how
to live with them.

the origin of "law"
where do laws come from?

From your earliest days, you came to understand there are certain rules to live by. You heard mom or dad say, "Don't touch that hot stove!", and it appeared that parents were the source of all the rules.

Then, as you grew older, you realized there is a larger world out there and there are other sources for the rules that govern your life. List some of those other sources:

_____   _____

_____   _____

_____   _____

But then comes the question: where do these people come up with all those laws? What is the ultimate source for the laws that govern your life? When you try to answer these kinds of questions, you are dealing with the worldview category of "Law."

God is the answer!

> The Christian believes that God has provided laws (and a means of discovering those laws) for mankind. "God is the only Legislator," says Carl F.H. Henry. "Earthly rulers and legislative bodies are alike accountable to Him from whom stems all obligation– religious, ethical and civil" (UTT, 259).

Henry mentions three areas in which God rules. Describe each one in your own words:

1) **religious:** _____

2) **ethical:** _____

3) **civil:** _____

When you combine these three areas of life, you are looking at ALL of life! There is no area that is outside of God's rule and domain. All is related to God.

check it out!

A law is a principle that always holds true.

defining "law": physical laws

"Law" simply refers to a principle that is always_____. For example, the "law" of gravity is a description of a principle built into the universe that causes objects to attract one another. Gravity works every time. It is a constant. In other words, it is an accurate description of **reality.**

week 8

week 8 day 1

If your friend says that he has decided to step off the top of The Empire State building, what would you tell him?

- [ ] You hope he has a nice flight.
- [ ] He is not living according to the real world.
- [ ] He is neglecting a basic principle of the universe, the law of gravity!
- [ ] He needs a "reality check"!

The last three statements would all be appropriate because your friend is about to suffer the consequences of living contrary to one of God's physical laws.

moral laws

During the week on Ethics, you discovered that the biblical view includes certain principles that govern our moral lives. And these laws are just as binding and unchanging as the laws in the physical world. Moral laws are a part of the real world, the "totality of reality."

> Society must decide whether an absolute legal standard exists. It does not matter whether society would prefer fixed or flexible laws; what matters is whether an absolute code is real. If such a code does exist, we, as mortals, must discover and obey it, for it points to a Law-giver worthy of our obedience and worship. The Christian, of course, believes such law and such a Law-giver exist (UTT, 260-261).

It doesn't matter if you like it or not, laws don't depend on "feelings." What does matter? _____

_____

_____

civil laws

A third area where God has established his rule is in the civil arena. As in the first two areas, the civil law code carries with it consequences for disobedience. Find Genesis 9:6, and respond to the following questions:

1) If someone commits murder, who is responsible for seeking justice?
   - [ ] God
   - [ ] Society
   - [ ] The physical world

2) What is the reason given for repaying the murderer in this way?

_____

The basis for punishing a murderer is the fact that all people are created in the image of God. As long as people are created in God's image, those that murder should be punished.

thinking like a christian

How long have people been created in God's image? _____
In the future, will people still be created in God's image? _____
What if someone lives in the deep jungles of South America; is he still
created in God's image? _____

When they are based on eternal moral principles, civil laws have an unchanging
foundation. They are just as real and constant as the law of gravity.

We see from all of this that the Bible explains why laws must exist. They exist
because man is in rebellion against God and His law, so earthly laws and means of
repayment are required to curb or neutralize that rebellion.

Meditate on the following passage as it relates to being accountable to God for obeying His laws on every level: religious, moral, and civil. What insights do you see
that encourage you to maintain a holy life style?

Hebrews 12:1-10: _____

_____

_____

_____

_____

day 1 summary:

> **Laws are descriptions of the way the world is designed to operate in every
> area of life: physical, moral, spiritual, and civil.**

week 8 key verse: **Colossians 1:17**
"He is before all things, and in him all things hold together."

note: The key verse for this week at first may not seem to relate to "law." But
when you think about it, the fact that Jesus Christ "holds together" everything is
itself the basis for "law." That's because laws "hold together" society. They keep
society from crumbling into chaos by making individuals accountable for their
actions. You'll learn more about this aspect of law as you continue this week's study.

looking for "law" in all the wrong places
what if man makes the rules!

From our study of Theology, we understand that "God rules." And because He rules, we have laws to live by. But to get a clearer picture of the significance of God's laws, let's take a look at law from another angle. We can do that by asking the question: **What if there were no God?**

If we start with the assumption that God does not exist, that would mean that all moral and civil laws come from our own minds. What would be the result of this "human-centered" system of laws? Read the next text box carefully:

"I make up my own rules."

> Systems which deny God as Law-giver ultimately fail and will always adversely affect every individual mired in them. They fail because they recognize neither the dignity of man created in the image of God nor the fallen nature of man. If God does exist and does create law, then any society that ignores His laws will be out of step with reality. Further, a society or state that forgets God will promote arbitrary laws, consequently causing its subjects to lose respect for the legal system. John Whitehead believes that when fundamental principles of law are undermined, "public confidence in law and public willingness to abide by law are also sapped.". . . . Without a law that is both unchanging and worthy of obedience, where can the individual discover a moral code (apart from mankind)? Man quickly realizes that if God does not exist, all things are permissible (UTT, 259-260).

The above paragraph states that "man-centered" systems of law will...
(check the right answer)

- ☐ ultimately triumph
- ☐ be a positive benefit to mankind
- ☐ be more in line with reality
- ☐ ultimately fail
- ☐ have a more stable basis than a God-centered system

"Man-centered" systems of law **will** always fail because of five specific reasons. Summarize in your own words the five reasons listed above:

1) _____

2) _____

3) _____

4) _____

5) _____

week 8

"Skip, you need a

'reality check'."

the law and **your worldview**

These negative consequences start when we deny that God is the source of all law. Let's take another look at each of these areas to see how they relate to the ten world-view categories. Use the following list and write the category in the blank that best corresponds to each phrase. However, this time we will state the phrases in a positive way: Sociology, Philosophy, Ethics, Theology, Psychology, Law, Politics.

"Acknowledge God as Law-giver"   _____

"the dignity of man...the fallen nature of man"   _____

"in step with reality"   _____

"respect for the legal system"   _____

"public willingness to abide by law"   _____

"discover a moral code"   _____

Check your answers:

God as Law-giver (**Theology**)

the dignity of man and fallen nature (**Psychology**)

in step with reality (**Philosophy**)

the legal system (**Politics**)

public willingness to abide by law (**Sociology/Law**)

moral code (**Ethics**)

Once again it becomes clear: a consistent worldview effects **every** area of life.

but are laws **"good"**?

Your friend next door has been looking over your shoulder while you were doing your journal on "Law." He says:

"O. K., O. K., I understand that we have all of these laws and everything, but I still don't have a very good feeling about "laws" in general. I mean, they are so restrictive. I want to be free! I want to be me! I want to express myself in whatever way I feel without all of these restrictions. Laws are much too confining!"

What would you say to your friend? _____

_____

Can you think of an example from real life to explain to your friend why laws are good for us? _____

_____

_____

There are negative consequences for disobeying God's laws and positive ones that comes to individuals and society when we obey them. When it comes to laws, "God knows best"!

responding to the God who is "there"

Based on our study so far, is there any doubt in your mind that Biblical Christianity paints for us a picture of the entire scope of reality and life?

Over and over again, we come back to the fact that the Bible relates to all of life. You can't get away from God! He is concerned in a loving way with every aspect of your life.

Read **Psalm 139** to catch a glimpse of how the author describes the wonder of knowing that God is there. Write about your thoughts and feelings that come from your knowing that God is concerned with all of your life:

_____

_____

_____

day 2 summary:

> When it comes to laws, "God knows best."

the nature of things

(NOTE: The following is not a trick question)

What is furry, eats nuts and has a bushy tail?

Write your answer here: _____

Did you get it right? Good for you! Give yourself a hand! I told you it was not a trick question.

Now, how did you know that it was a description of a squirrel?
(Go ahead, this is not a dumb question. Really think about it and write out your answer.)

_____

Did you write something like this: because all animals that are furry, eat nuts and have bushy tails we call "squirrels."

Right again? EXCELLENT!

What we have just done is to describe what is called the "nature" of a thing. In other words, you know what something is according to the things that are true about it. It's natural for squirrels to have bushy tails and eat nuts.

As we learned several weeks ago during our study of psychology, human beings have a "nature." There are certain things that are true for all humans. One thing that makes us uniquely human is our spiritual dimension.

check it out!

Laws are descriptions of the nature of things.

everything has a "nature"

In fact, *everything* has a "nature," not just squirrels and humans. It's the nature of birds to sing, and it's the nature of frogs to croak. It's in the nature of an apple tree to sprout leaves in the spring and produce apples in the fall. All of these things, and others, make up what we refer to as the "nature" of a thing.

What does all of this have to do with our study of "law"? Laws are simply descriptions of the _____ of things. During the 1700's, men began to write about these laws as "**natural laws**."

discovering natural laws

But the question naturally arises (it's in the nature of us humans to be curious and ask questions about the nature of natural laws!), how do we discover these "natural laws"?

> God revealed his law to mankind, generally, through natural law. Every person has a conscience–some inherent sense of right and wrong (UTT, 262).

Look up **Romans 2:14-15**. Paul writes that the Gentiles do not have the law, such as the Ten Commandments, yet, even non-Christians understand that certain things are right and certain things are wrong. How do they know?

- ☐ They read about it in the Bible.
- ☐ They are taught by their parents.
- ☐ They find out by "trial and error".
- ☐ They have a conscience.

Now turn to **Romans 1:18-22**. How does Paul describe "general revelation" in verse 20?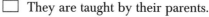

_____

Even though God made His presence known to man through nature (natural law), what was mankind's response?

_____

thinking like a christian

According to verses 21 and 22, by refusing to glorify and acknowledge God as the supreme ruler over life, man has suffered in what ways?_____

only **fools** reject **God's law**

> ...natural law explains why all men are considered accountable to God for their actions: because all men are aware of the existence of a transcendent law and still consciously disobey it (UTT, 262).

Read **Romans 1:24-32** for a list of some of the foolish behaviors people choose as a result of ignoring God's revealed laws. In what specific ways do you see these types of behaviors in your school, community or nation?

_____

_____

_____

_____

coming out of the darkness into **God's light**

1 Peter 2:9

But you are a chosen people, a royal priesthood, a holy nation, a people belonging to God, that you may declare the praises of him who called you out of darkness into his wonderful light.

"Only fools reject God's laws."

As a Christian, God has a better plan for you. Instead of living in spiritual and moral darkness, God has called you to a new life of freedom. What are the four phrases that God uses to describe you:

1)_____

2)_____

3)_____

4)_____

Why has He called you into his wonderful light?_____

_____

How can you "declare His praises" this week?

_____

day 3 summary:

Laws are descriptions of the "nature of things."

review key verse: **Colossians 1:17**
"He is_____ all things, and in him all things hold together."

God's laws are good for you

be careful how you drive!

Before anyone can drive a car he/she must demonstrate knowledge of the "rules of the road" by studying the "Driver's Manual" and passing a test. Driving down the "road of life" requires the same attention to the rules that govern life.

The Bible is God's "Driver's Manual" for life. In it God has given us the details for how we should live – the "rules of the road" for a safe and fulfilling life.

> God has made His law known to man through the Bible. Natural law provides man with a general concept of right and wrong, and then the Bible fleshes out this skeletal framework so that man may know what God considers lawful. (UTT, 262)

The Bible should not be viewed as just a boring old book of rules and regulations. The precepts in the Bible point the way to experiencing a healthy and happy life for the here and now! So fasten your spiritual seatbelt, and get behind the Scripture-wheel for the drive of your life! You are about to embark on a short joy-ride using the life-enhancing Road Map of Truth!

here's to your health!

example #1 : During the sixth and seventh centuries, leprosy began to spread widely in Europe. By the fourteenth century, the human death toll from leprosy had reached a terrifying peak.

What did the physicians of the day do to stop the ever increasing ravages of this disease? They thought that it was caused by eating hot food, pepper, garlic and the meat of diseased hogs.

As you might imagine, their remedies were of no use. About the same time, the Black Death began to ravage the land and took the lives of one out of four persons – an estimated sixty million. It is considered the greatest disaster of human history.

What brought an end to the major plagues of the Dark Ages? People turned to an idea they read in the Bible.[1] Look up **Leviticus 13:46** and summarize the answer that they found there: _____

_____

example #2 : Up until the late 1700's, it was the practice in most cities and towns to dump human waste into the streets. Yucky! Diseases like cholera, dysentery, and typhoid fever killed millions of people. Deliverance from these deadly epidemics only came when people began to apply two sentences from the Scriptures.[2]

thinking like a christian

What was this basic principle of hygiene mentioned in **Deuteronomy 23:12-13**?

_____

_____

example #3 : In the 1840's, Vienna was famous as a medical center. Yet in the maternity wards of a well-known teaching hospital, one out of every six women died from infection. A similar mortality rate was observed in every other hospital. It was customary for the doctors to begin each day by visiting the morgue to perform autopsies. Then, without washing their hands, they would go into the maternity wards to examine the women there.

A doctor named Ignaz Semmelweis noticed the problem and started washing his hands in a basin of water before examining each patient. He saw dramatic results almost immediately, with very few women dying from infection.

Yet, many centuries before Semmelweis, God gave to Moses very detailed instructions on how to handle the dead. The biblical procedure was even more specific than Semmelweis used, and more effective. What were the additional factors needed to keep infection from spreading?[3] Refer to **Numbers 19:16-19** as you answer the following:

> After touching a corpse, a person must. . .
> · _____ his clothes
> · bathe in _____
> · Wait for ____ days
> > . . . before being considered "clean."

These instructions are scientifically proven to deter the spread of infectious diseases. Yet these principles were written down by Moses over 3,000 years before modern medical "science"!

> **check it out!**
>
> **Modern medical science is catching up to what the Bible has said all along.**

the dark ages . . . past and present!

The reason that the "Dark Ages" are called "dark" is because the "light" of the Bible was not widely known. For the most part, folks did not have access to the Scriptures. If people had been following these instructions all along, millions of lives would have been spared a lot of misery!

But guess what? Even though most people have access to the Bible today, we are still experiencing certain health-related problems, even here in the United States. The next example explains why.

example #4 : AIDS is a current health problem that is spreading rapidly around the globe. HIV, the virus that leads to AIDS, is contracted primarily through sexual contact.

Did you realize that we already have the cure for the spread of HIV? It is a simple practice that, if everyone followed it, would stop the majority of AIDS cases from ever developing. Do you know what would stop the spread of the AIDS virus?

thinking like a christian

The answer, again, is found in the Bible. It was God's idea in **Genesis 2:24** that a man and a woman should be united for life. God's Road Map for Life goes on to warn about the dangers of sexual activity outside of a marriage covenant. For example, **1 Corinthians 6:18** says:

> Flee from sexual immorality. All other sins a man commits are outside his body, but he who sins sexually sins against his own body.

Do you realize that sexual sin is not only immoral according to God's law, but it is also against your own body? That's because over 30 different kinds of sexually transmitted diseases can cause some of the following physical problems: high fever, vomiting, severe abdominal pain, agonizing pains in the muscles of the arms and chest (lasting for hours), sterility, birth defects, brain damage, blindness, deafness, heart attacks, insanity, and oh yes, death!

Are you willing to take your chances on experiencing the above symptoms in exchange for a few moments of pleasure? Another thing you need to keep in mind is that sex outside of marriage goes against God's moral law. To commit sexual immorality is to invite God's judgement on your life.

God's view of sex!

Does this mean that God is down on sex? Not at all. God's Road Map is clear that sexual expression in marriage is designed to be a great joy and blessing. In fact, God suggests that a newly married couple take a **one year** honeymoon! (Check it out in **Deuteronomy 24:5.** And by the way, the translation "bring happiness to the wife" does not mean telling her jokes!)

God thought up the whole idea of sexual intimacy, and He knows how it works best. That's why He gave instructions for the most fulfilling way to experience His best: one man and one woman for life!

"A one-year honeymoon! God is too cool!"

taking the **driver's test**

Read through **Proverbs 3:1-8,** and make a list of the benefits of driving your life according to God's "rules of the road":

_____

_____

_____

day 4 summary:

> The Bible is God's "Driver's Manual" for life that points the way to experiencing a healthy and happy life.

week 8

can we legislate morality?
the law according to harry

Harry S. Truman, our 33rd President, had this to say about the origin of the laws upon which the United States of America was founded:

> The fundamental basis of this nation's law was given to Moses on the Mount. The fundamental basis of our Bill of Rights comes from the teaching which we get from Exodus and St. Matthew, from Isaiah and St. Paul. I don't think we emphasize that enough these days. If we don't have the proper fundamental moral background, we will finally wind up with a totalitarian government which does not believe in rights for anybody except the state.[4]

What connection does Truman make between the Bible, law, morality and government? _____

_____

_____

_____

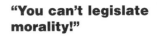

"You can't legislate morality!"

According to Truman:

Can you have government without morality? _____

Can you have morality without law? _____

Can you have law without the Bible? _____

While a society can have laws without the Bible, these laws would be man-made laws, and there would be no reason for people to obey the laws except to keep from being punished if caught.

On the other hand, the Bible gives a solid basis for truly moral laws. Government's role then is to translate those moral laws into civil law. So there is a direct link from the Bible to government, by way of natural law and biblical ethics.

week 8

a foundation for law

"ALL laws have a

moral foundation."

> For the Christian, law is grounded on the firmest foundation and therefore does not flex or evolve. . . . "Law has content in the eternal sense. It has a reference point. Like a ship that is anchored, law cannot stray far from its mooring." The Christian legal perspective creates a legal system that does not fluctuate according to the whims of man and, therefore, is more just (UTT, 261).

The text above comments on a certain quality of law. What is unique about the Christian legal perspective compared to other systems of law?_____

_____

What would make this system of law more just than other systems? _____

_____

_____

protecting human rights

> In one sense, law and morality are inseparable. When one declares theft illegal, one is making a moral judgment–theft is condemned as immoral, because it violates divine law. . . . Man must concentrate on formulating a legal system that legislates morality only to the extent that order is maintained and human rights are protected (UTT, 266).

Issues like abortion and homosexuality are more than just legal issues. They deal with more than a woman's rights or the right to privacy for two adults. The long-standing civil laws upon which these issues rest have traditionally been based on natural law.

But recently, some people have claimed that a woman has a "right" to her own body. Therefore, it is further claimed that she can abort a pregnancy if she desires. How would you evaluate this idea from a biblical worldview:_____

_____

> If, as the Bible claims, man is created in the image of God, then each human life becomes inestimably precious and meaningful. This, in turn, creates a firm foundation on which a system of human rights can be built (UTT, 265).

If human life is "inestimably precious," what does this imply about the abortion issue?_____

_____

week 8

Human rights are not founded on society's current ideas, but on the fact that people are created in the _____ of God.

But in recent years, these civil laws have been changing?
Why? _____

Our lawmakers are moving away from the biblical basis of natural law. Civil laws, ripped from their foundation, have been set adrift in a sea of relativity and human whims.

check it out!

If people are created in the image of God, that has serious implications for abortion.

action point

What can YOU do to stop this trend away from natural law?
Brainstorm on several things you can do:

_____

_____

_____

Share these ideas with a few close friends or church leader!

day 4 summary:

Laws based on the Bible have a "reference point," an absolute moral standard.

review key verse: **Colossians 1:17**
"He is before all things, and in him ____ _____ hold together."

thinking like a christian

Week 8 summary:

Another piece of the worldview puzzle falls into place: "Law." "Natural law" is the idea that God has created the universe to run on certain principles that are true for everyone and everything. These laws govern the physical universe as well as the moral, spiritual and civil areas of life. Laws are not to be avoided but are the rules to live by which are designed by God for our good and the good of society.

ENDNOTES
1. *None of the Diseases*, S.I. McMillen, Fleming H. Revell Co., Old Tappan, NJ, 1963, pp. 11-12.
2. Ibid., pp. 12-13.
2. Ibid., pp. 14-16.
4. *America's God and Country Encyclopedia of Quotations*, William J. Federer, Fame Publishing, Inc, Coppell, TX, 1994, pp. 589-590.

notes:

politics
everybody's got rights . . . right?

Why do some women abort their pre-born children? Because they claim a legal "right" to their own bodies. Why do some people try to stop the construction of a new dam? Because they claim that a small fish in one of the creeks has a legal "right" to its own habitat. Why do some people take the school district to court if a teacher has a Bible on his desk in the classroom? Because they claim a legal "right" to separate "church and state."

You read about it everywhere: Women's rights, gay rights, abortion rights, civil rights, animal rights. . . it seems that everybody and everything has rights! We hear so much about "rights," but what happens when someone else's "rights" step on your "rights"? And who's to say which "rights" are the right "rights"? With all this talk about "rights," where do "responsibilities" fit in?!

Only a Biblical Christian worldview can sort through the maze of "rights" in light of our "responsibilities." The answer to the "rights" issue is found in a biblical view of "Politics."

Politics, the art of governing a city, state, or nation, answers the question: **What is** ◄······ **the structure and role of government?** This week you will add another piece of the puzzle for a complete Biblical Christian worldview.

We will be dealing with some ideas that are controversial in our society today. That's because many people are moving away from a biblical understanding of these issues. But as always, we will seek out God's perspective and principles that will guide us into building the best political system.

During this week, look for
   . . . how God relates to government
      . . . how our human nature dictates what type of government is best
        . . . the purpose of government
          . . . why religion and politics DO mix, and
            . . . when you should obey the government and
              when you should not!

This week will put you on the right track to understanding what's wrong (and right) about rights.

week 9

government and god
there are only two things for certain!
(would you believe . . . three?)

The saying goes, "There are only two things for certain, death and taxes."

Well, actually, there are more than just two. We could add one more to that list: death, taxes, and **government!**

Why did we add "government"? Because "government" has been around as long as death and taxes! We usually think of death and taxes as something to be avoided. Does that make "government" as bad as the other two?

Our understanding of biblical sociology revealed that God established "the state" as one of the three main institutions of society. And the reason He did that is a **theological** one. "Government" is an expression of God's nature.

But how can government reflect the nature of God?

The next few pages will explore the connection between God and government.

"Keep God out of government!"

it all starts with God

In the first place, God is a God of "order." In other words, He always does things in an orderly manner. Examples of this are found throughout the Bible.

For instance, when God created the heavens and the earth, He did it in an orderly fashion. In fact, the universe is called the "cosmos." This is a Greek word that means "order." It is the opposite of "chaos," meaning "disorder."

Furthermore, God gave commandments for how we should "order" our lives morally. And in the New Testament, "order" was a concern of Paul.

Read **1 Corinthians 14:40**. What is the context of this verse?

_____

_____

it's time for a little order around here!

How does the Godly characteristic of "order" relate to government?
What do you think?

_____

_____

To help you to think about your answer, reflect on this: what if there were absolutely no government, no laws, no police, no courts, no common laws such as highway speed limits, no civil authority whatever. What would life be like? Check your answer:

- [ ] Cosmos
- [ ] Chaos
- [ ] Confining
- [ ] Cooperative

> Government should adhere to the principle, "Let all things be done decently and in order" (1 Corinthians 14:40; Exodus 18:19f) since this is a reflection of God's character, and it should be participatory, so that Christian citizens can better influence the state to conform to God's will as a social institution (Proverbs 11:11) (UTT, 295).

Government is necessary to keep individuals from infringing on the rights of others. Therefore, government is . . . (check the right choice)

- [ ] A "necessary evil" in the world.
- [ ] An after-thought of God.
- [ ] A positive good for mankind.
- [ ] Neither positive nor negative; it just is!

Government, as a reflection of God's nature, is designed to be a positive good for man by seeking to keep order in society so people can live peaceful and tranquil lives. But there is a second relationship between God and government.

seeking justice

The idea of "justice" comes from the nature of God. It was discussed under theology when the question was asked: What is God like? Which of the three major characteristics of God relates to God's justice?

- [ ] God is Ruler
- [ ] God is Relational
- [ ] God is Righteous

wow!

"Do not deny justice to your poor people in their lawsuits." Exodus 23:6

Being just, or righteous, is a central aspect of God's character. God's justice means that He always judges fairly. And He requires that we reflect His nature in being just with our fellow man, too.

> Most everyone believes that furthering justice is an important task of the state, but the Christian sees justice as the principal reason for the state's existence. Such a view of justice can follow only from a view grounded on an absolute guarantor of unalienable rights. Because the Christian view is based on such a foundation, promoting justice becomes more important than any other aspect of government (UTT, 298).

week 9

pause to reflect

Reflect on **Exodus 23:6,** and list some reasons why justice is an important aspect of government. _____

_____

_____

_____

day 1 summary:

> **God designed government to bring order to society and to promote justice.**

> **week 9** key verse: **Colossians 3:25**
> "Anyone who does wrong will be repaid for his wrong, and there is no favoritism."

government and man

a tale of **two islands**

Imagine that you are responsible for governing the inhabitants of two islands. On one island, Island "A," you have people who are good, hard-working, family oriented, and honest. On the other island, Island "B," the people are violent, lazy and greedy.

As you look into the future, which of these two islands would you predict would have the greatest prosperity and individual freedom?

☐ Island "A"
☐ Island "B"

Which of the two islands will require the most laws, policemen and prisons?

☐ Island "A"
☐ Island "B"

Based on the above scenario, summarize your thoughts on why both God and government are needed: _____

_____

_____

_____

why we need government (part 2)

Yesterday the connection was made between God and the need for government. Government is a reflection of God's character, specifically His O_____ and J_____ .

But government not only reflects the character of God, it also must conform to the nature of man.

government and human nature

> Perhaps the Christian concept America's founders best understood was the Christian view of human nature. The United States was born in an environment in which men held a Christian view of man's fallen nature, but they did not forget that man was created in the image of God. These two beliefs about man have profound implications for a Christian view of politics, which is reflected in America's founding fathers' attempts to tailor a government suited to man's place in God's creative order (UTT, 296).

America's founders had a unique opportunity to design a totally new political system. As they began their task, they took seriously the biblical worldview of "Psychology." What two aspects to human nature did they consider important?

       1) Mankind is created in God's _____ .

       2) Mankind has fallen into _____ .

These ideas concerning man's basic nature provided the foundational principles for our national government: a government that, while far from perfect, has proven to give more freedom and opportunity to its citizens than any other nation in history.

"If men were angels, no government would be necessary."
James Madison, our 3rd President (UTT, 296)

human rights . . . and responsibilities!

> The fact that these unalienable rights have an unchanging Source is crucial for Christian politics. If man's rights were not tied inextricably to the character of God, then human rights would be arbitrarily assigned according to the whims of each passing generation. Rights are "unalienable" only because they are based on God's unchanging character. God established government to secure these rights. This protection of human rights is God's basic purpose for government (UTT, 297).

Think about it: all rights come from _____. Since human rights come from God, they are "unalienable," which means that only _____ can change them or take them away.

thinking like a christian

But if God is the source of our rights, He is also the source of our "responsibilities." These are the moral standards which must guide our day-to-day lives and decisions.

Our founding fathers understood well this connection between God, man and government. Read the following quote from James Madison, signer of the *Declaration of Independence* and the main author of the U. S. Constitution:

> We have staked the whole future of the American civilization, not upon the power of government, far from it. We have staked the future. . . upon the capacity of each and all of us to govern ourselves, to control ourselves, to sustain ourselves according to the Ten Commandments of God.[1]

does it still apply today?

James Madison said that we need to control ourselves according to the Ten Commandments, yet some people today say that the Ten Commandments should not even be posted on the walls in a public school. What do you think about that?

_____

_____

Some people say that a woman has a "right" to her own body. Therefore, she has the "right" to abort an unwanted child. How would you evaluate this from a biblical worldview? _____

_____

_____

If accepting Jesus Christ as one's personal Savior and Lord leads a person to accept his responsibility to obey God's laws, and obeying God's laws leads to good government, what can you do to promote good government?

_____

_____

_____

day 2 summary:

Government is necessary because of man's sinful nature.

the purpose of government

Godly government

A key passage that outlines the purpose of government is found in **Romans 13: 1-7**. Find that section in your Bible, and fill in the following blanks:

- This passage mentions two ways that the state is to function. In verses 3-4, what are these two ways?
  1) To _____ those who do right.
  2) To _____ those who do wrong.

- These two basic functions of the state, to commend the good and punish the evil, come from the _____ which God has established. (verse 1)

- Because state authorities are established by God, we should _____ to them. (verse 5)

- Submitting to government means to give what is due to those that rule, including _____, _____, _____, and _____. (verses 6-7)

From a biblical perspective, the purpose of the state is to punish those who break the law and praise those who do well. Evaluate your local, state or national government by listing how they are fulfilling these two functions. NOTE: Check your local newspaper for examples:

An example of government punishing an evil-doer is:

_____

_____

An example of government praising someone who does good is:

_____

_____

a good question

Thus, government protects mankind from its own sinful nature. But who protects the society from the sinful inclinations of the men who make up the government? This was the problem with which America's early leaders grappled in attempting to create a just political system (UTT, 296).

thinking like a christian

This brings up a very sticky problem: if people are our rulers and people are basically sinful, then who "protects the society from the sinful inclinations" of those who rule?

How did America's early leaders solve the problem?

_____

_____

The founding fathers built into our Constitution a unique system that kept people in power for only short periods of time and allowed for the smooth transition of power to new leaders.

In that way, power is not concentrated with just a few people. And since government leaders are elected by the people at large, those leaders have an obligation to rule fairly or they will be dismissed.

the fourth branch of government

> The aspects of American government that most closely conform to the Christian ideal are, not surprisingly, the most valuable part of America's political heritage. These include America's division of governmental power into three branches, legislative, executive, and judicial, and the concordant system of checks and balances (UTT, 296).

You are aware of the "three" branches of government, but you might say there are actually "four" branches that make our government function properly? What is the fourth branch of our government? _____

It is "We, the people. . .!" Yes, the citizens of the United States act as a fourth branch of government. Our role is to elect godly leaders and hold them accountable for their actions by either continuing to re-elect them or vote them out of office. We have the ultimate obligation to "check" and "balance" the power of our elected officials.

the scope of government

> Government, according to [the Biblical Christian] view, has limited responsibility. The state should concentrate on enforcing justice and avoid meddling in other institutions' business. It must never assume the responsibilities of other institutions, including church and family (UTT, 298).

Limited government was the vision of the early leaders in America. The state should stick to its purpose and not interfere in the affairs of _____ or _____. This allows the maximum amount of freedom for all people.

Evaluate the current situation here in America. Does the state interfere with areas that belong to the church or family? If so, in what ways?

government and you

What can you do to help make our government function in the way that God designed it to work?

day 3 summary:

Because mankind is sinful, government needs to be limited in scope and balanced in power.

week 9 memory verse: **Colossians 3:25**

"Anyone who does wrong will be_____ for his wrong, and there is no favoritism."

the making of the constitution

The men who founded our nation were in a unique position. They had the opportunity to start a new government from scratch. Before them was a blank piece of paper and the history of man's efforts to govern himself.

If you had been one of the delegates to the Constitutional Convention back in 1787, what principles would you have written into the Constitution?

religion and the founding fathers

The founders of the United States designed the federal government to operate according to certain principles. Did they intend for religion to play a part in this great "experiment in freedom"? What do you think?

"The founders of the U.S. were all Deists, not Christians."

☐ Yes, the founders saw the importance of government being founded on specifically Biblical Christian religious principles.

☐ No, the founders meant to separate the state from religion.

☐ The founders thought that religion should be a personal, private belief but not play any role in running the country.

The following is a <u>brief</u> summary of some of the thoughts and opinions of these original founders. Can religion be separated from government? Their words give the answer.

George Washington (1732-1799) was President of the Constitutional Convention and the First President of the newly formed United States of America. He said during his Farewell Address after his second term in office. . .

> Of all the dispositions and habits which lead to political prosperity, religion and morality are indispensable supports. . . .[2]

According to Washington, what are the two necessary supports of any political system?

☐ _____

☐ _____

"Popular government" refers to our political system where people vote for their officials. What is necessary for this type of government?

_____

Why do the people who make up a nation need to be moral?

_____

Patrick Henry (1736-1799) helped write the Constitution of Virginia, was a member of the Continental Congress, and a five-time Governor of the State of Virginia. Look at his words:

> It cannot be emphasized too strongly or too often that this great nation was founded, not by religionists, but by Christians; not on religions, but on the Gospel of Jesus Christ. For this very reason peoples of other faiths have been afforded asylum, prosperity, and freedom of worship here.[3]

The U.S. was not founded on just any religion, but on the _____ religion. Yet this has not led to narrow-minded religious bigotry toward other religions. What has been the result, according to Henry? _____

_____

Thomas Jefferson (1743-1826) was the primary author of the *Declaration of Independence* and our 3rd President. He wrote in 1781. . .

> God who gave us life gave us liberty. . . . Indeed I tremble
> for my country when I reflect that God is just; that his justice
> cannot sleep forever.[4]

Jefferson mentions two things about God. First, God is the source of _____.
And second, God is _____.

Liberty and justice are two key goals of government. Is Jefferson saying that a
nation cannot have liberty or justice apart from God?

John Quincy Adams (1767-1848), at the age of fourteen, was appointed by
Congress as Ambassador to Russia. He also served as a U.S. Senator, U.S. Minister
to France and Britain, Secretary of State for President James Monroe and as the 6th
President of the United States. On July 4, 1821, he said in a speech. . .

> The highest glory of the American Revolution was this;
> it connected in one indissoluble bond the principles of
> civil government and the principles of Christianity.[5]

What does "indissoluble" mean? _____

According to John Quincy Adams, what two things are inseparable?

---

you can't have one without the other . . .

By now you should have a pretty good understanding of the relationship between
religious principles and politics. Write a short summary based on the ideas of the
founders:

_____

_____

_____

_____

day 4 summary:

> You can't have a system of government without religious ideas. Our
> founding fathers based their ideas for government on a biblical worldview.

a question of obedience

what would you do?

You are living in Germany during the 1940's. The government has ordered all Jews to be taken away from the city and sent to "death-camps." Your best friend, who is a Jew, comes to your door one night and asks to come in. She tells you that her parents, brothers and younger sister had been picked up by the secret police that afternoon while she was away from the house. She doesn't know what to do, where to go, who to trust.

What do you do? Read **Romans 13:5** and **Acts 4:19** before selecting one of the following options:

☐ Help her by hiding her in your basement.
☐ Tell her to go somewhere else.
☐ Call the secret police to report where she is.

Did you struggle with the two passages from the Bible? There seems to be a conflict: Do you obey the government according to Romans 13:5, or do you disobey the government as Acts 4:19 suggests? How do you know which command in the Bible to obey when the commands seem to contradict each other?

the "greater command" principle

The solution to the dilemma is found in **Matthew 22:37-39**. Jesus said that the _____ command is to love God, and the _____ is to love your neighbor. This suggests that some commands take priority over others.

Obey the greater command.

Jesus establishes the principle of the "greater command." In other words, when there is a conflict between two commands in Scripture, you should obey the "greater" one.

In the following examples, determine which is the "greater" command to obey.

Two nations are at war. A woman living in a town controlled by the corrupt government is hiding some spies from the other nation. Military officers come to her door and ask if she knows where the spies are hiding. What should she do?

☐ Colossians 3:9 says to not lie, so she should tell the truth by showing the authorities where the spies are hiding.

☐ Exodus 20:13 says to not murder, so she should lie to the authorities in order to save the lives of the spies.

(See Joshua 2 and Hebrews 11:31 for the correct answer to the real-life situation with Rahab.)

thinking like a christian

The government passes a law to control the population growth. Nurses are ordered to kill certain newborn babies and allow others to live. What should the nurses do?

☐ Romans 13:5 says to submit to civil authorities, so they should kill the newborns. They won't be held accountable by God because they were just obeying orders.

☐ Exodus 20:13 says to not murder, so the nurses should not kill any of the babies, and if necessary, lie to the government to conceal their actions.

(See Exodus 1:15-20 for the historical event behind this dilemma involving the King of Egypt and the Hebrew midwives.)

You can see from these two biblical examples that the greater principle is to save a life, even if it means disobeying civil authorities.

This demonstrates how a consistent worldview helps you to understand how to handle life's situations. Here we combined "Ethics" (how we determine the moral thing to do) with "Politics" (how we relate to government) and arrived at the answer to our initial dilemma regarding hiding our friend from the Nazis.

you and government

> . . . the Christian is called to obey government, to honor justice, and to preserve order. However, this does not mean that Christians must obey government blindly. The political leader has a responsibility to God, and the Christian must hold him accountable (UTT, 300).

Proverbs 29:2 is very instructive regarding your responsibility as the fourth branch of government. Summarize the verse in your own words:

_____

_____

day 5 summary:

If there is a conflict between what the government says and what God says, the "greater command" principle of Scripture directs us to obey God.

review key verse: **Colossians 3:25** "_____ who does wrong will be repaid for his wrong, and there is no favoritism."

week 9 summary:

The starting point for every political system is its religious foundation, which ties together theology and philosophy. The purpose of the state is to bring order to society and to administer justice, which assumes certain ethical standards. Psychology relates to politics because man's sinful tendencies require a balance of power in government. A biblical sociology determines that the state has a limited function and should not interfere with the family and the church. And lastly, natural law and the Bible are the basis for making the laws of the land. It all forms a consistent and total picture–a biblical worldview of politics!

ENDNOTES
[1] *America's God and Country Encyclopedia of Quotations,* William J. Federer, Fame Publishing, Coppells, Texas, 1994, p.411.
[2] *Original Intent,* David Barton, Wallbuilder Press, Aledo, Texas, 1996, p.116.
[3] *America's God and Country Encyclopedia of Quotations,* William J. Federer, Fame Publishing, Coppells, Texas, 1994, p.289.
[4] Ibid., p.323.
[5] Ibid., p.18.

notes:

economics
making money by the bible!

Don't let the term "economics" fool you. It may sound a little stuffy, but it deals with an area that is near and dear to your heart. Very simply, it has to do with how you get what you want and keep what you get! It is how we exchange goods and services.

Have you ever thought about how the economy in America works and how it is different from other nations of the world? We enjoy a standard of living that is the highest in the world. And it's not just because we have more natural resources. Other countries have basically the same resources we have in North America, but their people live in relative poverty. Why the difference?

It's because the founders of our nation used biblical principles in establishing how people could make and use money. Their Biblical Christian worldview informed their economic principles.

"Economics" comes from the Greek; "*ecos*" = house and "*nomos*" = law. It is the "law of the household." Our earlier study on law showed us that God designed the universe to work according to certain laws or principles. This is true for the world of nature (physical laws) and our ethical behavior (moral laws).

But also, there are economic principles that determine the best way to "get what we want." Based on the nature of God (He is Just) and the nature of man (made in God's image, yet sinful), a picture of the these basic economic principles begins to emerge.

The main principle of biblical economics is "free exchange." That means that people should be free to produce things (legal things, of course) and sell things as they choose. History has proven that "free and peaceful exchange" (also called a "free market") allows the greater amount of material wealth and well-being for the greatest number of people than any other system of economics.

This week you'll be introduced to
   . . . practical lessons on work from the "Seven Dwarfs"
      . . . the Bible's view on "Big" government
         . . . the need to own things
            . . . and other practical tips on God's view of money and
               Godly living.

So don't let it fool you. Economics plays an important part in your worldview. Thinking like a Christian means understanding economic issues.

work is a way of life
lessons from the seven dwarfs

Remember Snow White and the Seven Dwarfs? It's a great story! For the moment, zero in on those little guys, the seven dwarfs. With a whistle and a song, they would "Hi-ho" to work in the mine each day.

What can we learn about work from the seven dwarfs? Give it a shot:

_____

_____

check it out!

> **Work is a natural and necessary part of life . . . so you might as well enjoy it!**

Actually, those little story-book characters can teach us a couple of things.

The first thing is this: each day it's "off to work we go." Work is a _____ and necessary part of life. It's a daily routine for all of us in some form or another.

And second, since work is unavoidable, you might as well _____ it! You might not feel like whistling while you work, but it sure does make the time go better.

Know what? These two ideas come right out of the Bible!

a biblical view of work

Way back at the beginning of human history, God placed Adam and Eve in a beautiful garden. Think about it; when was the idea of "work" first introduced to mankind?

_____

Some people associate work with God's punishment for Adam after he sinned, but the Bible actually paints a different picture. Turn to **Genesis 3:17-19** and answer the following questions:

What was the consequence of Adam's sin?

_____

God's curse on the ground meant that it would now produce what?

_____

What words are used to describe Adam's labor?

_____

So is "work" God's curse on mankind?

_____

Actually, "work" is not the curse. Check out **Genesis 2:15**. Here it says that God placed Adam in the garden to "_____ it and take _____ of it."

Notice, this is *before* Adam sinned! Work was a part of God's original plan, His "good" plan for Adam even before his fall. God designed life in such a way that we are involved in His creation. A theologian once said, "God even milks the cow through you."

So work is not a curse. It is a part of God's blessing and design for mankind. We are designed to work. Only after the fall did this blessing become a hardship.

wow!

"God even milks the cow through you."

work has its rewards

> After casting man out of Eden, God decreed that mankind must face a life of toil (Genesis 3:17-19). But God, in His mercy, allowed that men who conscientiously adhere to this duty may be rewarded with private property. Proverbs 10:4 states, "Lazy hands make a man poor, but diligent hands bring wealth." God has designed a world in which the existence of private property encourages men to be fruitful (UTT, 327).

Look at **Proverbs 10:4** and re-write it in our own words:

_____

_____

Does this mean that everyone who works hard will become "wealthy"?

_____

The Bible does not promise lots of material riches, but it does convey the idea that we should keep what we earn. This is an important idea and will be explored more on Day 2.

but do i have to like it?

Do you have to "like" work? Of course not! But since it's a way of life, you might as well enjoy it. Look over the following verses to get God's perspective on work. Write your thoughts that come from each passage.

Exodus 20:9-11 - _____

_____

_____

Deuteronomy 16:13-15 - _____

_____

_____

Deuteronomy 24:19 - _____

_____

_____

Proverbs 12:14 - _____

_____

_____

Proverbs 21:25 - _____

_____

_____

putting it all together

What can you conclude from today's study regarding the biblical view of making a living? Write a summary:

_____

_____

day 1 summary:

Work is part of God's original plan for mankind.

week 10 key verses: Colossians 3:23-24
"Whatever you do, work at it with all your heart, as working for the Lord, not for men, since you know that you will receive an inheritance from the Lord as a reward. It is the Lord Christ you are serving."

private ownership
molly's question

You could always count on Molly to make things interesting, and this particular morning was no exception. The Tuesday Morning Bible Club had been studying the book of Acts. Molly wanted to say something, so in her customary way, she blurted out, "I've got a question! Jesus' disciples living in Jerusalem shared everything they had, right? So why don't Christians do that today? If we're really serious about following the Lord, why don't we form a commune and share everything in common?!"

Everyone in the Bible study just sat there in silence not knowing exactly how to respond. What do you think about Molly's question? Should Christians refuse to own anything privately and instead share everything like one big family? How would you respond to Molly?

christianity and socialism

> Christians are divided on the issue of economics. While many Christians believe the Bible encourages a system of private property and individual responsibilities and initiatives (citing Isaiah 65:21-2; Jeremiah 32:43-4; Acts 5:1-4; Ephesians 4:28), many others are adamant in their support for a socialist economy (citing Acts 2:44-45) (UTT, 325).

It turns out that Molly is not alone. There are some Christians today who call for a "socialist" system where everyone shares equally in the economic "pie." They advocate for centralized government planners to regulate the way people work and do business in order to distribute the wealth more evenly for all citizens.

Do you see how easy it is to link economic ideas to political ideas? You can't separate the two. As we are seeing throughout this study, each category fits into a larger picture for a total worldview.

Since economics and politics are inseparable, it is natural to talk about them together. So our question is now between two options:

Should the government be in control of the way people make and use their resources, property, or money (a system called socialism or communism)?

or

Should the government protect economic freedom to peacefully exchange goods and services (called a free market or capitalism)?

the bible and **private property**

Look at **Acts 2:44-45** where it describes how the first Christians lived together. Is this a pattern that we should follow today? _____
Why or why not? _____

_____

As it turns out, the passage in Acts 2 is a special situation with Jews coming to Jerusalem from every known nation (Acts 2:5). Notice how the Christians took care of each other: (Circle the word that best fits in the blank.)

First, the early believers _____ sold some of their property (some still had houses, see Acts 2:46) and pooled their resources. ("voluntarily" / "under compulsion")

Second, there was _____ government agency forcing anyone to contribute. ("no" / "a big")

Third, this was an illustration of Christian _____ rather then government welfare policy. ("charity" / "coercion")

What do you conclude about what this passage teaches concerning private property?

_____

check it out!

Private property refers to anything that a person owns, not just land.

private ownership: a biblical overview

But there is even a broader understanding about God's view on private property. Check out the following:

1 Kings 4:25 says that each man lived under his own _____ and _____ _____.

Jeremiah 32:44 indicates a future time when the nation of Israel will be free to _____ and _____ property. Private property refers to anything that a person owns, not just land.

Acts 5:1-4 Was Peter angry because Ananias owned property or because he lied about what he had?

_____

What is your conclusion about God's view of private property? Check your answer:

☐ God's design is for people to share all things in common.

☐ It's not clear from the Bible what we should do related to private ownership.

☐ The biblical view indicates that people have the right to own things privately and exchange them peacefully and freely.

thinking like a christian

practical christian principles

The United States was founded on the biblical principles of a free market and private ownership. This has led to building a nation whose people have one of the highest standards of living compared to other nations.

Following Christian principles has practical benefits. Look in the paper for examples of people living in socialist-controlled countries, and compare their situation with that of people living in free market economies. What factors contribute to whether people prosper or live in poverty? (Hint: Do people work harder when they are: A) Allowed to keep the fruit of their labor, or B) Required to place their earnings in a common storehouse?) _____

_____

_____

If you are involved in a group study, bring your articles to the next meeting and discuss the implication with your friends.

day 2 summary:

Biblical economics support private ownership.

stewardship
the bible and stewardship

Yesterday's Journal entry considered the biblical view of "private property." There is another side to that coin, and that is stewardship. Read the following text box for insight into this important concept.

> Beisner states, "Biblical stewardship views God as Owner of all things (Psalm 24:1) and man individually and collectively as His steward. Every person is accountable to God for the use of whatever he has (Genesis 1:26-30; 2:15). Every person's responsibility as a steward is to maximize the Owner's return on His investment by using it to serve others (Matthew 25:14-30)" (UTT, 327).

Read **Psalm 24:1.** Everything belongs to _____. Think of the world as God's "garden" and us as the managers of it. We are accountable to Him for how we use His natural resources and for what we produce with our work.

We all work in His garden, either directly or indirectly. What types of work would be direct involvement in God's garden?

_____

Direct involvement would include things like farming and raising animals. But it would also be the use of natural resources, which includes various kinds of technology, manufacturing and production (like construction, clothes, cars, and computers). These activities take the natural resources found in God's world and reshape them for our comfort and convenience. In other words, all legal and moral activities that better the human condition.

Indirect involvement in God's garden would be the services associated with the above activities. This would include such work as insurance, sales, business management, education, etc.

money is **soooooo convenient!**

So you are involved in God's garden one way or the other. In either case, in today's economy, you earn money for your work. Money is simply a convenient means of exchange for acquiring material things that other people work to produce. Therefore, how we spend money reflects how we manage the resources God has provided for us to use.

Money acts like a spiritual thermometer.

money is a **spiritual thermometer**

Jesus told a story about using money wisely, but He had a spiritual purpose behind the story. Read the entire parable in **Matthew 25:14-30,** and reflect on the following questions:

Who does the master represent? _____

If God is the master, who are the servants? _____

If we are the servants, what do the "talents" represent?

_____

If the talents relate to the things that God has given us, such as personal abilities that we can use for His Kingdom, what is the main point that Jesus is making in this story?

_____

Jesus is making the connection in this story that money acts like a spiritual thermometer. A thermometer gives an objective way to determine someone's temperature. In a similar way, Jesus is saying that how you make and spend money and how you use your God-given abilities are objective ways to determine your spiritual condition.

How are you doing with the wise use of the abilities that God has given to you? _____

What can you do this week to be a more faithful steward in God's kingdom?

_____

_____

applying God's wisdom to your life

God's wisdom book has tons of practical ideas on how to handle your money. Turn to **Proverbs 22** and write each idea in your own words:

vs. 1 - _____

vs. 2 - _____

vs. 7 - _____

vs. 9 - _____

day 3 summary:

Since we are "stewards" of our material possessions, how we use our money reflects our spiritual life.

---

review key verses: **Colossians 3:23-24**

"Whatever you do, work at it with all your heart, as working for the _____, not for men, since you know that you will receive an inheritance from the Lord as a reward. It is the _____ Christ you are serving."

 **social justice**

rich man, poor man

Molly, the girl in the Tuesday morning Bible study, still wasn't satisfied. She went on, "You know, the Bible says that we should love and care for one another, especially the poor. Look at all of those wealthy millionaires and big corporations that make all of that money. It's not fair. Wouldn't it be more compassionate to pass laws to tax the rich so the government can provide ways to help the poor?"

How do you respond this time to Molly's question? _____

"You tell'em, Molly."

You have to admit that Molly has a point. What could be more noble than helping the poor? Should Christians strive for "economic equality"?

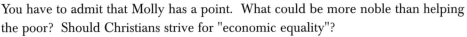

week 10

141

thinking like a christian

Good questions! Let's look for some answers from God's "Road Map" for life.

economic equality: a noble notion?

How does Paul's example and command in **2 Thessalonians 3:7-13** relate to the issue of whether we should seek "economic equality"?

_____

_____

If a person is able to work and doesn't, then he does not deserve to eat! That may sound harsh, but let's see how this plays out from a biblical worldview.

worldview analysis

What have you learned so far that would help you evaluate Paul's principle of "earning what you eat"?

All the pieces of a biblical worldview fit together.

(Theology) God's Righteous nature includes the quality of "justice." He is always fair. Is it fair to tax the wealthy to feed the poor? Why not?

_____

(Psychology) Considering that people are basically sinful, how would you expect them to act under a system of welfare?

_____

(Politics) Should the government take money from some people in order to give it to others? What's the biblical purpose for government?

_____

(Sociology) If government is not designed to redistribute wealth, then what social institutions do have the responsibility for looking after people in need?

_____

(Economics) Now consider what the Bible has to say about God's design for "work" from the study on Day 1. Who is responsible to work for what they have?

_____

This worldview summary shows that many principles converge to give a clear picture of this issue. Paul's admonition holds true: "If a man will not work, he shall not eat."

the "robin hood" syndrome

But aren't we supposed to help the poor? You know, like Robin Hood in the days of yore—take from the rich and give to the poor?

Sounds good, but God has a better plan for helping the poor. Check it out in **Leviticus 19:9-10.**

> How does the type of assistance mentioned in these verses give a sense of dignity to the person being helped?

> _____

> How does this plan benefit the owner of the fields?

> _____

> How is this biblical plan for helping those in need different from many government–run "welfare" programs used today?

> _____

God did not design "welfare" for people in need. Instead, you might call this the first "workfare" program. In God's economy, people are instructed to work for a living. God's provision of "gleaning" allows a person in need to work for themselves and gather their own food. In **Ruth 2:1-23** we see a real-life example of this principle in action! Read it for yourself.

This same theme is repeated in the New Testament. See **1 Timothy 5:8** and write out the warning connected with the importance of looking after your own family:

_____

_____

causes of poverty

What can you do to reduce poverty? Read **1 Timothy 6:17-19** to find out. (By the way, compared to the rest of the world, you are "rich"! So these verses apply to you, too.)

> Based on 1 Timothy 6:17-19, list some of the attitudes and actions that will put you in a position to help the poor:

> 1) _____

> 2) _____

> 3) _____

day 4 summary:

All who are able should work for their food. People who are unable to work should be cared for by their families and the church.

economics and freedom
freedom or security?

The year is 2025, and there is a national poll being taken to determine the economic direction of our nation. You must decide between the following two options.

1) **freedom:** You will be free to live where you want to, choose your own work and own your own things.

2) **security:** You will be assured food, shelter and a guaranteed job arranged by the government.

What are the positive and negative points for you and for society of choosing **freedom**?

Positives: _____

Negatives: _____

What are the positive and negative points for you and society of choosing **security**?

Positives: _____

Negatives: _____

If you had to choose one, which would it be? (circle your choice)

freedom   **security**

Clearly, there is a relationship between the type of economy a society chooses and the amount of freedom the individual must sacrifice. In a socialist society, the individual must relinquish to the government much of the control over his life. "The only way to arrive at equal fruits is to equalize behavior," says Beisner; "and that requires robbing men of liberty, making them slaves" (UTT, 331).

According to Beisner, if you choose security over freedom, you lose your liberty and become a _____ to the state.

economic freedom leads to political freedom

Economic freedom and the right to private property are crucial for political freedom (UTT, 331).

Restate in your own words how these three areas inter-relate: economic policy, personal freedoms, and politics.

_____

_____

_____

As we discovered during our journey into politics, it's in the nature of governments to control people. That's why our founders sought to reign-in the potential for abuse by the state by creating separate branches of government.

But there are two other ways government is kept in check.

One is economic freedom. Economic freedom allows the development of private institutions, such as businesses, universities, and civic associations. These are important because they help disperse the ability of a too-powerful state to control people.

the role of private property

Also, private property is important to hold the state in check. How does private property have the result of balancing the power of government?

_____

_____

Think about it: if you can buy a printing press or TV station or sell newspapers, you have the opportunity to tell other citizens about what government officials are doing. If elected officials become corrupt or try to take too much power, then a "free press" can report this, and the offending politicians can be voted out of office.

But what would happen if there were no private property and the government owned all the printing presses and TV stations and controlled what news was distributed?

_____

_____

wow!

Private property leads to a free economy that supports a free people!

This is exactly what happened in Nazi Germany during WWII. The people of Germany and the rest of the world did not know that Hitler was sending Jews to death camps until toward the end of the war. This is because there was no free press; Hitler controlled the news media.

So you see the importance of a biblical worldview that connects economic freedom, private property and political freedom.

putting the **pieces together**

How does **Ephesians 4:28** summarize the principles that you have learned about a biblical view of economics?

_____

_____

_____

day 5 summary:

Two economic features help to keep the abusive power of government in check: economic freedom and private property.

review key verses: **Colossians 3:23-24**

"Whatever you do, _____ at it with all your heart, as working for the Lord, not for men, since you know that you will receive an inheritance from the Lord as a _____. It is the Lord Christ you are serving."

week 10 summary:

When it comes to economics, God has the best ideas. First of all, God has designed us to work. Even though work may be difficult because of Adam's sin, we can still enjoy being involved in God's garden. Secondly, through work we gain possessions that we can use to freely and peacefully exchange for other things that we need. The biblical worldview directs us to a free market system that allows the greatest personal freedom to make and spend money and improve our own economic situation. And third, we should be willing to share our abundance and experience with those who need to learn to help themselves. Give someone a fish and he is fed for a day; teach someone to fish and he's fed for a lifetime.

notes:

 # history

dry bones or dynamic ideas

"Don't know much about history" –that's a line from a song from the sixties. It could be the theme song for many students today. The reason that history seems so boring is because the focus is usually on names, places and dates. But these are only the dry bones of history. Do you know what is the real flesh and blood that brings life to those dry bones? The lifeblood of history is "ideas." That's right, ideas!

Once you grasp a worldview about ideas, history comes alive with relevance. Why? Because the ideas that people have do not change over time. The details change, the technology changes, but the basic ideas remain the same.

The Apostle Paul writes that the events of the Old Testament "happened to them as examples and were written down as warnings for us. . ." (1 Corinthians 10:11). We can learn valuable lessons from the experiences of others.

But more than that, **a Biblical Christian worldview gives us a context for understanding history.** The Bible points to a definite progression of events. A story-line that begins in the "beginning," flows through time and climaxes at the resurrection of Jesus. Even our calendars attest to the change from B.C. (Before Christ) to A.D. (Anno Domini, meaning "In the year of our Lord").

The Bible also points to the future, a time when God will draw to a close this earthly story and bring into account the lives and actions of all men and women. Then, there will be a new heaven and a new earth, harmony and peace.

Don't know much about history? Maybe now you will be motivated to dive into the world of ideas as you read about the past. This week will help you take the plunge. Go ahead, dive in!

christianity and history

baloney detectors

We all know that baloney is not "real" meat. It is just beef parts that are cooked up and mashed together. In other words, it's a cheap imitation of the real thing.

In the same way, some ideas are "baloney," cheap imitations of the truth. The apostle Paul talked about detecting "baloney" ideas when he said in **Colossians 2:8**,

> **See to it that no one takes you captive through hollow and deceptive philosophy, which depends on human tradition and the basic principles of this world rather than on Christ.**

Hollow ideas. Deceptive philosophies. They're just a bunch of baloney—cheap imitations of the truth.

The world is a war-zone of ideas. Hostile worldviews are competing for your allegiance. As in any war, the choices are rather basic: either be captured, or take captives.

"Time to turn on your baloney detector!"

taking thoughts captive

The next time you hear someone claiming that something is true, you need to turn on your "baloney detector." Try your "baloney detector" on the following idea:

> Don't talk to me about your religion. You just accept everything on "blind" faith!

BUZZZZZ! There it went. What did your baloney detector pick up in those lines?

_____

_____

what do you mean . . .?

By now you should have a pretty good understanding of why you believe what you believe. When someone challenges your faith in God, the first thing you should do is to ask them a simple question, like: **"What do you mean by 'faith'?"**

Usually, they will define "faith" as a "blind acceptance of something for which there is no proof." But is that the basis of biblical faith? Give an answer based on what you have learned during your journey into a biblical worldview:

_____

_____

Christians believe the basis for their entire worldview appeared in human history in the form of Jesus Christ about two thousand years ago. While "Christ died for our sins" is solid orthodox Christian theology, "Christ died" is history (UTT, 357).

Think about it: "Christ died" is _____. The entire Christian worldview stands or falls on events in history: specifically the life, death and resurrection of Jesus Christ. If those historical events are not true, then there is no Christianity! That is why it's so important to add the category of "history" to our total picture of the world.

The study of history is not optional for the Christian; it is _____. And just because this category is last in our line-up does not mean that it's less important than any of the other categories.

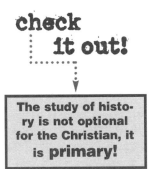

check it out!

The study of history is not optional for the Christian, it is **primary!**

history and the Bible

The Christian also believes that the Bible is God's revealed Word in the form of a trustworthy book grounded in history. Thus, for the Christian, history is supremely important. Either Christ is a historical figure and the Bible is a historical document that describes God's communications with man and records events in the life of Christ, or the Christian faith is bankrupt (1 Corinthians 15:14) (UTT, 357).

According to the above text, what two things would render the Christian faith bankrupt?

1) _____

2) _____

If our Christian faith means anything, then it must rest on the fact of Jesus' life, death and resurrection. But how do we know that Jesus died? Because the Bible is an _____ document.

Turn back to Week 3, Days 3 and 4 and review the specific reasons for the Bible being trustworthy. In those two lessons, seven reasons were given. List them here in the margin ···▶

no baloney

A biblical worldview gives a solid basis for knowing what is true and what is not. With a trustworthy Bible as the foundation, you won't be captured by "baloney" ideas.

The Bible says a lot about how its truth relates to your life. Read **Psalm 119: 30-35,** and turn the words of these verses into a prayer from your heart to God.

day 1 summary:

A Christian's faith is based on actual historical events, not just "blind" acceptance.

week 11 key verse: **Colossians 3:4**
"When Christ, who is your life, appears, then you also will appear with him in glory."

the bible and history
one very important question

When considering the claims of Christianity, one question must be asked immediately: Can we trust the Bible to tell us the truth about God's actions in history (UTT, 358)?

Think about it; you are basing your whole life and future (eternity is a long time!) on what some book says! Maybe you had better be very sure that book is a reliable source.

Yesterday you reviewed several reasons why the Bible is true. Today, we will zero in on three areas that are important in judging the accuracy of the Bible from a historical perspective.

"Right on, Prof!"

the question of "authorship"

Who wrote the Bible? If you take a religion course in most universities today, the professor will tell you that the book of Matthew was not written by one of Jesus' apostles, but by some unknown scribe who had not known Jesus personally. How would you respond to the professor's remarks?

_____

_____

If you were sitting in class when the professor made that remark, it would be a good time to bring out your baloney detector! The professor just made a truth-claim about the Bible. He claimed that the Bible is not to be trusted because it was written long after the events actually took place. If this were true, then, according to the professor, there would be time for myths to creep into the story in the re-telling of it before it was written down. But is that how the Bible was written?

thinking like a christian

Today's scholars have little doubt that the books of the Bible were written largely by eyewitnesses. William F. Albright, a leading twentieth-century archaeologist writes, "In my opinion, every book of the New Testament was written by a baptized Jew between the forties and the eighties of the first century (very probably sometime between about A.D. 50 and 75)" (UTT, 358-9).

Why is it important that the Bible was written by "eyewitnesses"?

_____

eyewitnesses in the new testament

List the reasons that each of the following writers of the New Testament is a reliable source of information about the life, works, death and resurrection of Jesus.

Peter: **2 Peter 1:16-19** - _____

John: **John 21:20-25** - _____

Luke: **Luke 1:1-4** - _____

Paul: **1 Corinthians 15:3-8** - _____

and **Galatians 1:18-19** - _____

It takes more than twenty or thirty years for legends or myths to develop. The evidence points to the conclusion that the history in the Bible was written by men living during the time of Jesus!

but what about those copies?

As it turns out, archaeology (the science of digging up facts from history) has consistently confirmed that the Bible is a trustworthy historical document.

When the Bible mentions names and places and dates, archaeological discoveries confirm those names and places and dates! Can you trust a historical document like that?

headline news

Read the following newspaper article, and write a headline that would catch people's attention.

The Daily Times

HEADLINE_____

A bit of mystery surrounds the discovery of the Dead Sea Scrolls in 1947. Some claim that the young man who found the first cave containing ancient Bible manuscripts was a simple shepherd; others suggest that he may have been involved in a smuggling operation. Regardless of his occupation, his discovery rocked the archaeological world.

One of the first Dead Sea Scrolls reproduced almost the entire book of Isaiah, in a manuscript more than 1,000 years older than what was previously thought to be the oldest

manuscript. Incredibly, this ancient text was virtually identical to the modern Hebrew book of Isaiah!

This discovery, along with the subsequent discovery of fragments of almost every Old Testament book in nearby caves, reinforced the Christian assertion that the Bible is a trustworthy historical document that has not been corrupted by copyists. The Dead Sea Scrolls, and all relevant historical evidence, support the belief that the Bible provides an accurate account of actual people and events (UTT, 361).

something to **get excited** about!

It's been said that the heart cannot rejoice in what the mind rejects! Is your heart rejoicing? Are you excited about being a Christian? If not, maybe it's because your mind has been taken captive by some hostile ideas concerning the historical reliability of the Bible.

Spend a few minutes considering the evidence presented in today's session. Pray that God would confirm in your mind the trustworthiness of His Book, and then allow your feelings to express real excitement over the fact that you are basing your life on the truth!

day 2 summary:

Archeology confirms that the Bible is a trustworthy historical document.

thinking like a christian

jesus and history

it sounds like a squirrel to me

A ten year old boy was asked by his Sunday School teacher to name something that is brown, furry and eats nuts. The boy thought for a moment and said, "I know the answer is Jesus, but it sure sounds like a squirrel to me!"

Of course, that is just a joke but not too far from the truth. It seems like the answer to any question asked in Sunday School is always "Jesus," "God," or "the Bible."

By now you realize that when it comes to a biblical worldview, the answer really is Jesus! In fact, Christian theologians agree that Christianity stands or falls on one thing. Can you name that one, specific thing that undergirds all of Christianity?

_____

_____

the resurrection factor

Jesus' _____ is the key to everything else. **This is a major issue for the Christian! So major, in fact, that it sets Christianity apart from every other religion.**

check it out!

Jesus' resurrection is the key to Christianity.

Jesus, a great moral teacher, but . . .

Because of the centrality of Christ's resurrection, opponents of Christianity have tried to deny that Jesus historically rose from the dead. Walk onto most university campuses in America today, and you will hear professors of religion say something like this:

> Jesus was a great moral teacher but he was not God.
> Jesus did not come back from the dead; it was just his
> teachings about loving others that "came alive" in the
> hearts of his followers.

Any baloney going on there? How do you respond to comments like these?

_____

_____

_____

We have already discussed the trustworthiness of the Bible and the fact that the New Testament was written by eyewitnesses of the life of Jesus or individuals close to the actual eyewitnesses.

But who, exactly, were these eyewitnesses? What did they have to say about the resurrection? And why did they say it? Knowing the answer to these questions will help you respond to skeptics who reject Jesus being God.

eyewitness testimony

> The resurrected Christ was witnessed by more than 500 people (1 Corinthians 15:6), including Mary, Peter, and ten other apostles. These witnesses were so moved by the resurrection that they committed their lives to it and to the One whose divinity and righteousness it vindicated . . . If the disciples did not consider the resurrection a historical event, is it really conceivable that they would be willing to die for this kind of testimony (UTT, 360-361)?

What is in **1 Corinthians 15:3-8** that leads you to conclude that Jesus was physically raised from the dead? _____

List the individuals or groups of people who saw the resurrected Jesus:

1) _____
2) _____
3) _____
4) _____
5) _____
6) _____

Think about Jesus' disciples; what kind of men were they? (Look up **John 20:19 & 25**)

_____

After the resurrection, how did they change? (see **Acts 4:18-21 & 5:17-21**)

_____

What did they claim made the difference in their attitudes and actions?
(Look at **Acts 4:8-13**)

_____

Based on the historical fact of the resurrection of Jesus, how sure are you about your faith in Christ? (Mark the following "Assurance" scale)

0%   50%   100%

> The faith of modern-day Christians should be no less secure than that of the apostles because it is grounded in historical fact. This fact forms the basis for the Biblical Christian worldview and the Christian philosophy of history (UTT, 361).

applying **his**tory to **your** story

Is your faith secure? Is it based on the facts of history? Is there any reason for not believing the testimony of the disciples?

Take a few minutes in prayer to thank God for making Jesus' resurrection a solid historical fact; a fact so secure that you can trust your life with it.

day 3 summary:

> The eyewitness accounts by the disciples give historical assurance that Jesus was bodily raised from the dead.

> **review** key verse: **Colossians 3:4**
> "When _____, who is your life, appears, then you also will appear with him in glory."

history and you
history with a purpose

Have you ever asked the question: What is my purpose in life? This question, when asked on a personal level, actually assumes a more basic question: Is there any purpose to life in general? In other words, does God have a plan and purpose for history?

A biblical worldview informs us that God has a plan. This plan for humanity is played out through the events that have happened in the past and includes what is taking place today and even what is happening in the future. And His wonderful plan also includes YOU!

> This belief about God's actions in history has vast ramifications for mankind. If the Christian philosophy of history is correct, then not only is the overall story of mankind invested with meaning, but every moment that man lives is charged with purpose (UTT, 362).

"Every moment that man lives is charged with _____." Do you believe that? Is your life charged with purpose?

Let's get a biblical perspective to that last question concerning purpose in life. To do that, we have to step back and take a "Big Picture" view of God's purpose for His creation. Then, from that vantage point, we can focus on His purpose for your life.

the **big** picture

First, the "Big Picture." Read the following from **Acts 17:**

> **26** **From one man he made every nation of men, that they should inhabit the whole earth; and he determined the times set for them and the exact places where they should live.**
> **27** **God did this so that men would seek him and perhaps reach out for him and find him, though he is not far from each one of us.**
> **28** **For in him we live and move and have our being.**

Who is the "one man" Paul refers to in verse 26? _____

What is the point Paul draws from the fact that Adam is the first man?

_____

Verse 27 gives a purpose statement when it says, "God did this so that. . .". What is the "so that"? In other words, why did God determine the times set for each man? _____

_____

What is the conclusion found in verse 28? _____

_____

Fill in the blanks to amplify verse 28:

for in Him (God)
  we (Paul, you and everyone else)
    live (_____)
      and move (_____)
        and have our being (_____)

more meaning for your life!

From the Christian perspective history is a beautiful unfolding of God's ultimate plan for mankind. Does this mean, however, that only the future holds any value for the Christian? Does the Christian worldview destroy the role of the present in history? The answer is a resounding no. In the Christian view, God is active throughout history; therefore, this perspective creates more meaning for every moment of time . . . (UTT, 362).

History is simply the progression of time. You are currently living in real time. God is active right now! He has a plan and purpose for **your** life. As you follow His plan, take on "more _____ for every moment of time...."

check it out!

By understanding a biblical worldview you will gain a better understanding of how you fit into God's plan.

What is God's plan for your life? Do you realize that He has already revealed His purpose and plan for you? It involves all the principles and ideas found in the Bible. This study of a Biblical Christian worldview has introduced you to many of the purposes and plans that God has in all areas of life.

For example, in the area of **Theology**, you learned that God is relational. Based on that fact, what is God's plan for you regarding your relationship to Him? In simple language, God's plan is for you to enter into a relationship with Him by accepting Jesus' payment for your sin problem.

In **Philosophy** you realized that you can know what is true in the world by studying God's general revelation (His World) and His special revelation (His Word). In light of this, what should be one of your goals in life? _____

_____

The section on **Biology** demonstrated that you are a created being, which gives significance to your life because _____

_____

Biblical **Ethics** revealed that God has established certain moral guidelines for life. How does that intersect your life? _____

_____

Mankind is created in God's image, yet is fallen into sin, according to Christian **Psychology**. This idea relates to you in what two ways?

  1) _____
  2) _____

The family is a significant part of God's plan according to a biblical **social** worldview. What does that imply about God's plan for your life?

  ☐ Marriage is optional.
  ☐ Living together without being officially married is
      O.K. as long as we love each other.
  ☐ Being married and raising children are probably in
      my future, so maybe I need to start now to prepare
      myself for being a partner and parent.

What is the main point of biblical **Law,** and how does that apply to you?

  Main point: _____

  Application: _____

Does God have a plan for **Politics**? If so, how should you relate to this system of government? _____

In the area of **Economics**, God's will for your life revolves around how you make and spend money and use other resources. So what?

_____

If God has revealed Himself and His ways throughout **history**, what does that imply about how well you do your history homework and raise issues in class from a biblical worldview?

_____

personal application

Since God has a special place for you based on His overall purpose, spend some time praying for His wisdom to understand how you fit into His plan.
(See **James 1:5**)

day 4 summary:

History is the unfolding of God's plan and purpose for mankind, and that includes YOU!

the direction of history
invasion of the . . .

Alien invasions have been a popular theme of Hollywood film-makers over the years. If someone asked you, you could probably name your favorite "alien" movie.

But there is another type of invasion that is not science fiction. Instead of fictional aliens, this other invasion is real. In place of a sinister attack on mankind, this invasion has had a lasting, positive impact on the human race. Not only that, but there is a second invasion that is scheduled to take place in the future. This future invasion will also have an effect of "world-changing" proportion. Can you name each of these two invasions?

Past invasion: _____

Future invasion: _____

The two invasions refer to a time when the supernatural invaded the natural world. It has happened once already when God became a man and walked this planet. The birth of Jesus Christ marked the first invasion. The second divine invasion will take place in the future when Jesus comes again to establish His kingdom on planet earth.

direction, what direction?

This Christian belief about the direction of history is known as a linear conception of history. That is, Christians believe that human history had a specific beginning (creation) and is being directed by God toward a specific end (judgment), and that historic events follow a nonrepetitive course toward that end (UTT, 363).

check it out!

> The linear concept of history means that history is going in a straight line. It is headed in a certain direction.

What does "linear" mean? _____

Although God is in control of the direction of history and will bring it to an end, the Bible also makes it clear you have a part in the process. You can make choices affecting your life and your future.

what the future holds

Some people consult the "Psychic Hotline" to try to peer into the future. But Christians have something better. God has told us what the future has in store.

For the Christian, history is moving toward a specific climax: the Day of Judgment (Acts 17:31; Romans 2:11-16). At this point, Christ's victory over sin will become apparent to all, and Christians throughout history will be allowed to share in His triumph (UTT, 362-363).

How will we share in His triumph? Read the exciting details concerning Christ's victory in **1 Corinthians 15:51-57**. Write any thoughts or questions you have from reading these verses:

_____

_____

_____

a new home. . . right here on planet earth

There is something else that God has in store for us in the future. Read **2 Peter 3:13-14** to find out what it is.

History reaches its climax when God judges sin and establishes a new _____ and new _____.

The book of Revelation describes this as our new home where we will dwell eternally with Him in peace and splendor (See **Revelation 21 - 22**). What a beautiful ending to the story of history. It began at creation and ends with a re-creation of a place for all believers to live.

We are living
between the two
invasions.

living between the two invasions

While the new earth will be a wonderful place, there is still a lot of "living" to do in the here and now. When you consider the time-line of history, we are living between the two invasions of Jesus' first and second coming. Can we know what to expect during this "in between" time? What should we be doing? A biblical world-view of history gives us the answers.

Read **Matthew 13:24-30** as you ask yourself the question, "What will life be like between Christ's first and second coming?" What did you find will take place during this "in between" time?

_____

_____

growing weeds in God's garden

In **Matthew 13:36-43**, Jesus explains that two things will be growing at the same time. First, his church will grow as Christians go into all the world and share the good news of God's love and forgiveness. This represents the _____ growing in the field.

But what about the weeds? They represent non-Christians who will also increase during this age. However, there will be a time in the future when God will judge the world and remove those who do evil.

Since this "in between" time in history will see the growth of evil in the world, should we just resign ourselves to the fact that evil will increase and not try to do anything about it? Or is there a better course of action for Christians to take?

what to do?

Again, God has given us His directions on what we should be doing during this "in between" time. Read **Titus 2:11-14**. What is our responsibility before the end will come?

_____

_____

_____

_____

it makes a difference in your life

> Christian history centers in the reliability of the Bible. . . . If this historical perspective is correct, then the entire Christian worldview is proved to be true, and it follows that knowing, accepting, and following Jesus Christ as Savior and Lord is the most important thing anyone can do. Wise men still seek Him, and for good reason. He gives meaning to history, and to life (UTT, 363-364).

What is the most important thing a person can do? _____

Why is knowing and following Jesus Christ as Savior and Lord so important?

_____

In what ways do you plan to follow Jesus as Lord?

_____

_____

day 5 summary:

History has a direction; it moves in a straight line from the creation of the original heavens and earth to the new heavens and new earth.

review key verse: **Colossians 3:4**
"When Christ, who is your life, appears, then you also will appear with him in
_____."

 **week 11 summary:**

Christianity is a historical religion. It is the story of God's dealing with humanity from the creation of time to the climax of His judgment and re-creation of a new heaven and new earth. The story of the Bible has been found to be reliable everywhere it touches historical people, places and events. The most significant event recorded in the Bible is the resurrection of Jesus Christ. Because of Jesus' death and resurrection, we can have assurance of God's love and acceptance by placing our complete trust in Him as our substitute for sin. That assurance should make a difference in how we live each day of our lives.

a final challenge
biblical christianity in retreat

This course of study has taken you through a Biblical Christian worldview. But as you look around, you will notice that our society is moving away from Christian principles in every area that we have studied.

> The Christian worldview is in retreat in nearly every arena of American life including our universities, media, arts, music, law, business, medicine, psychology, sociology, public schools, and government. "The humanistic system of values has now become the predominant way of thinking in most of the power centers of society," claim James C. Dobson and Gary L. Bauer. According to Dobson and Bauer, the Christian worldview has only two power centers remaining in America- the church and the family, and both of them are under tremendous pressure to surrender (UTT, 401).

"God wants you to make a difference in your world."

What are the signs of our time that indicate that Christianity is in retreat in some of the areas listed above? _____

_____

_____

According to James Dobson and Gary Bauer, what is the predominate worldview in our country today? _____

Humanism is a religious system of thought that starts with man instead of God. It is a total worldview that comes in three forms that are prominent in western civilization:

    -- Secular Humanism,

      -- Marxism-Leninism, and

        -- Cosmic Humanism (New Age).

These humanist philosophies seek to tear down the biblical foundations that have supported our nation for over 300 years. The break-down of society is a result of the influence of these non-Christian worldviews and the retreat of the church in society!

As you consider all the problems that our country faces today, do you want to be a part of the problem, or a part of the solution?

_____

what's a body to do?

There are some things that you can do to have a positive impact on our culture and our world.

> What are we to do? Go on the offensive! Light a candle. Pray (2 Chronicles 7:14; Colossians 1:9-14). Study (2 Timothy 2:15). Understand the times (1 Chronicles 12:32). Rebuild the foundations (Psalm 11:3). Spread the word. Truth is our greatest weapon (UTT, 401.)

So don't just sit there, **do something!** How do you go on the offensive without being "offensive"? List each of the above suggestions, and prayerfully add a specific thing that you can do to make it a reality in your life:

1) Light a candle: (what can you do in a positive way to make a difference in your school or community?)

    _____

2. ____: For what, specifically? _____

    _____

3. _____: You could start by purchasing the book, *Understanding the Times** which is the basis for this Journal. Or go to Summit Ministries web site (the address is at the end of this section) for a suggested reading list.

4. _____ the times: (What can you do to be better informed about the ideas and trends in our culture? See * below.) _____

    _____

5. Rebuild the _____: (Before you can rebuild the foundations, you must understand the ideas that our society is founded upon. How can you do that? When will you do it?) _____

    _____

    _____

6. _____ the word: (Make a list of people close to you who need to hear the word.)

    _____
    _____
    _____
    _____
    _____
    _____

making it happen

Why not share this list with some friends who can pray with you. Make them a supporting team to help you accomplish your action points!

a closing prayer

As a closing prayer for this entire study of a Biblical Christian worldview, meditate on **1 Peter 3:15,** and sincerely ask God to bring to mind what you need to do in preparation for confronting our world with the truth of God's Word:

> **But in your hearts set apart Christ as Lord. Always be prepared to give an answer to everyone who asks you to give the reason for the hope that you have. But do this with gentleness and respect. . .**

check it out!

We recommend the abridged version for high school students and the original book for college students and adults.

* To better understand the times, you should purchase a copy of David Noebel's book, **Understanding The Times**, by calling Summit Ministries Bookhouse at (719) 685-9103 9AM - 5PM CST. This book will give you more information on how the Bible relates to all of life and will introduce you to three major worldviews that are influencing our society today: Secular Humanism, Marxist/Leninism, and Cosmic Humanism (the New Age movement).

Also, call for a brochure to attend a **Christian Leadership Conference** held each summer. This life-changing two-week program will teach you to champion the truth of Christianity with meaning and purpose. See the last page of this Journal for more information about this mind-expanding opportunity.

Summit Ministries equips servant leaders to understand worldview analysis, trains them to champion the Christian worldview, and inspires them to love God with their hearts and minds. For over 35 years, Summit Ministries has helped Christians to avoid being captured by false and deceptive philosophies (Colossians 2:8), and encouraged them to take captive every thought for Christ (2 Corinthians 10:5).

for more information, write or call:
Summit Ministries
PO Box 207
Manitou Springs, CO 80829
(719) 685-9103

check us out on the web at:
http://www.summit.org

we welcome your comments regarding the student journal:
info@summit.org

Student's Guide to the Fact Sheets

In this section, we've provided you with Fact Sheets on a variety of topics, complete with key quotes and sources for more information. Our hope is that these fact sheets will become a good basis for your term papers and essays.

As You Use These Fact Sheets, Keep a Few Things in Mind:

■ *These Fact Sheets are Just a Start.* We've begun the research work, but haven't done it all for you! Hopefully, these quotes and sources will get you started, but none of the lists are meant to be comprehensive – there's always more good stuff out there!

■ *Finding the Other Good Stuff.* When you've looked up the books on these lists, turn to the back and look at the bibliography and end notes to find out who the author is using for information. Then, look up those books! Write to the organizations listed and ask them for more information; talk to people who know about your subject and ask for references. Each source should lead you to other sources.

■ *Getting Great Quotes.* Your most powerful quotes will come from people who shouldn't be saying what they are saying. (This is particularly important when you're writing for a non-Christian instructor.) For example, a quote by an evolutionist saying the fossil record doesn't support evolution is more powerful than a similar quote from a creationist.

■ *Credibility.* Make sure the people you quote and the sources you use have the greatest credibility possible. Go to original sources whenever possible – don't simply quote Christian authors talking about what other people think.

■ *Use Discretion.* Don't assume that an author is a Christian just because we have them on our Fact Sheets, or that Summit Ministries would agree with everything that person has said or written. In some cases, we've quoted sources that we definitely disagree with so you can see what another viewpoint is saying.

Abortion
UNDERSTANDING THE TIMES

Key Quotes

"Many people are very, very concerned with children in India, with the children of Africa where quite a few die of hunger, and so on. Many people are also concerned about all the violence in this great country of the United States. These concerns are very good. But often these same people are not concerned with the millions who are being killed by the deliberate decision of their own mothers. And this is what is the greatest destroyer of peace today – abortion, which brings people to such blindness."
Mother Teresa, quoted in Cal Thomas, "Meek Mother Teresa delivers a verbal knockout punch,"
Colorado Springs Gazette Telegraph, 9 February 1994, B7.

"'The nurses have to look at the ultrasound picture to gauge how far along the baby is for an abortion, because the larger the pregnancy, the more you get paid. It was very important for us to do that. But the turnover definitely got greater when we started using ultrasound. We lost two nurses – they couldn't take looking at it. Some of the other staff left also.' What about the women having the abortions? Do they see the ultrasound? 'They are never allowed to look at the ultrasound because we knew that if they so much as heard the heartbeat, they wouldn't want to have the abortion.'"
Dr. Joseph Randall, who performed over 32,000 abortions, quoted in David Kupelian and Mark Masters,
"Pro-Choice 1991: skeletons in the closet," *New Dimensions*, September/October 1991, 43.

"The fact that restricting access to abortion has tragic side effects does not, in itself, show that the restrictions are unjustified, since murder is wrong regardless of the consequences of prohibiting it; and the appeal to the right to control one's body, which is generally construed as a property right, is at best a rather feeble argument for the permissibility of abortion. Mere ownership does not give me the right to kill innocent people whom I find on my property, and indeed I am apt to be held responsible if such people injure themselves while on my property. It is equally unclear that I have any moral right to expel an innocent person from my property when I know that doing so will result in his death."
Prochoice philosopher Mary Anne Warren, "On the Moral and Legal Status on Abortion," in *The Problem of Abortion*,
2d ed., ed. Joel Feinberg (Belmont, CA: Wadsworth, 1984), p. 103, quoted in Randy Alcorn,
Pro Life Answers to Pro Choice Arguments, (Portland, OR: Multnomah Press, 1992), p. 86.

"A nurse who had worked in an abortion clinic for less than a year said her most troubling moments came not in the procedure room but afterwards. Many times, she said, women who had just had abortions would lie in the recovery room and cry, 'I've just killed my baby. I've just killed my baby.'

"'I don't know what to say to these women,' the nurse told the group. 'Part of me thinks "Maybe they're right."'"   Diane M. Gianelli, "Abortion providers share inner conflicts," American Medical News, 12 July 1993, 36.

Key Sources

Alcorn, Randy. *Pro-Life Answers to Pro-Choice Arguments*. Portland, OR: Multnomah, 1992.
> *This is the KEY book on this topic, pulling together resources from many others. Also includes extensive appendixes of organizations and pro-life resources.*

Ankerberg, John, and John Weldon. *When Does Life Begin?* Brentwood, TN: Wolgemuth and Hyatt, 1989.

Beckwith, Francis J. *Politically Correct Death: Answering Arguments for Abortion Rights*. Grand Rapids, MI: Baker Books, 1993.

SUMMIT MINISTRIES

FACT SHEET

Summit Ministries
does not necessarily endorse all the views and
ideas represented by these sources.

PO BOX 207
MANITOU SPRINGS, CO 80829
(719) 685-9103

Gianelli, Diane M. "Abortion providers share inner conflicts." American Medical News, 12 July 1993, pp. 3, 36-37.

Grant, George. *Grand Illusions: The Legacy of Planned Parenthood.* 2nd ed. Franklin, TN: Adroit Press, 1988, 1992.

Kasun, Jaqueline. *The War Against Population: The Economics and Ideology of Population Control.* San Francisco, CA: Ignatius Press, 1988.

Key Organizations

National Right to Life
419 Seventh St., Suite 402
Washington, D.C. 20004

Christian Action Council
701 W. Broad St., Suite 405
Falls Church, VA 22046

WEBA (Women Exploited By Abortion)
Route 1, Box 821
Venus, TX 76084
(214) 366-3600

Key Verses

Genesis 1:27
Exodus 20:13; 21:22,23
Psalm 139:13-16
Proverbs 24:11,12
Jeremiah 1:5

Creation

UNDERSTANDING THE TIMES

Key Quotes

"The essential point of creation has nothing to do with the timing or the mechanism the Creator chose to employ, but with the element of design or purpose. In the broadest sense, a 'creationist' is simply a person who believes that the world (and especially mankind) was *designed*, and exists for a *purpose*."
Phillip E. Johnson, *Darwin on Trial*, (Downers Grove, IL: Inter Varsity Press, 1991), p. 113.

"Science is possible only because we live in an ordered universe which complies with simple mathematical laws. The job of the scientist is to study, catalogue and relate the orderliness in nature, not to question its origin. But theologians have long argued that the order in the physical world is evidence for God. If this is true, then science and religion acquire a common purpose in revealing God's work."
Paul Davies, *God and the New Physics*, (New York: Simon and Schuster, 1983), p. 144.

"[A]t this moment it seems as though science will never be able to raise the curtain on the mystery of creation. For the scientist who has lived by his faith in the power of reason, the story ends like a bad dream. He has scaled the mountains of ignorance; he is about to conquer the highest peak; as he pulls himself over the final rock, he is greeted by a band of theologians who have been sitting there for centuries."
Robert Jastrow, *God and the Astronomers*, (New York: W.W. Norton, 1978), p. 116.

"A science which deals with origin events does not fall within the category of empirical science, which deals with observed regularities in the present. Rather, it is more like a forensic science, which concentrates on unobserved singularities in the past. That is, a science about origins is a singularity science about the past; it differs from a scientific understanding about singularities in the present. A science about the past does not observe the past singularity but must depend on the principle of uniformity (analogy), as historical geology and archaeology do."
"Just as a forensic scientist tries to make a plausible reconstruction of an unobserved (and unrepeatable) murder, so the evolutionist and creationist attempt to construct a plausible scenario of the unobserved past singularities of origin. So neither view is operation science. Rather, both are in the domain of origin science."
"Some events of origin may have nonnatural primary intelligent causes. But to insist on finding a natural cause where there is evidence for primary intelligent causes is like demanding that a geology class remain at Mount Rushmore until it discovers some natural process of erosion to explain the faces formed on the mountainside."
Norman L. Geisler and J. Kerby Anderson, *Origin Science: A Proposal for the Creation-Evolution Controversy*, (Grand Rapids, MI: Baker Book House, 1987), pp. 14, 25, 30.

Key Verses

Genesis 1:1
Genesis 1:27
Mark 10:6
John 1:1-3
Colossians 1:16,17
Hebrews 11:3

SUMMIT MINISTRIES

FACT SHEET

Summit Ministries
does not necessarily endorse all the views and
ideas represented by these sources.

PO BOX 207
MANITOU SPRINGS, CO 80829
(719) 685-9103

Key Sources

Bauman, Michael, ed. *Man and Creation: Perspectives on Science and Theology.* Hillsdale, MI: Hillsdale College Press, 1993.

Geisler, Norman L., and J. Kerby Anderson. *Origin Science: A Proposal for the Creation-Evolution Controversy.* Grand Rapids, MI: Baker Book House, 1987.

Johnson, Phillip E. *Darwin on Trial.* Washington, DC: Regnery Gateway, 1991.

Lester, Lane P., and Raymond G. Bohlin. *The Natural Limits To Biological Change.* 2nd ed. Dallas, TX: Probe Books/Word Books, 1989.

Moreland, J. P., ed. *The Creation Hypothesis: Scientific Evidence for an Intelligent Designer.* Downers Grove, IL: Inter Varsity Press, 1994.

Taylor, Paul S. *Origins Answer Book.* Mesa, AZ: Eden Productions, 1991.

Key Organizations and Publications

Origins Research, a quarterly published by Students for Origins Research, PO Box 38069, Colorado Springs, CO 80937-8069.

Institute for Creation Research, 10946 Woodside Ave. N., Santee, CA 92071.

Key Creationists

Kurt P. Wise
Hugh Ross
Duane Gish
John Morris
Henry Morris
Charles Thaxton

Reliability of Scripture

UNDERSTANDING THE TIMES

Key Quotes

"The earliest preachers of the gospel knew the value of...first-hand testimony, and appealed to it time and again. 'We are witnesses of these things,' was their constant and confident assertion. And it can have been by no means so easy as some writers think to invent words and deeds of Jesus in those early years, when so many of His disciples were about, who could remember what had and had not happened....

"And it was not only friendly eyewitnesses that the early preachers had to reckon with; there were others less well disposed who were also conversant with the main facts of the ministry and death of Jesus. The disciples could not afford to risk inaccuracies (not to speak of willful manipulation of the facts), which would at once be exposed by those who would be only too glad to do so. On the contrary, one of the strong points in the original apostolic preaching is the confident appeal to the knowledge of the hearers; they not only said, 'We are witnesses of these things,' but also, 'As you yourselves also know' [Acts 2:22]. Had there been any tendency to depart from the facts in any material respect, the possible presence of hostile witnesses in the audience would have served as a further corrective."

F. F. Bruce, *The New Testament Documents: Are They Reliable?*, 5th ed.
(Downers Grove, IL: Inter Varsity Press, 1960), pp. 45-46.

"There is no body of ancient literature in the world which enjoys such a wealth of good textual attestation as the New Testament."

F. F. Bruce, *The Books and the Parchments*, Rev. ed., (Westwood: Fleming H. Revell, 1963) p. 178.

"There is, I imagine, no body of literature in the world that has been exposed to the stringent analytical study that the four gospels have sustained for the past 200 years. This is not something to be regretted: it is something to be accepted with satisfaction. Scholars today who treat the gospels as credible historical documents do so in the full light of this analytical study, not by closing their minds to it."

F. F. Bruce, "Foreword," in *The Historical Reliability of the Gospels*,
Craig Blomberg, (Downers Grove, IL: Inter Varsity Press, 1987) p. ix.

"Skepticism toward the reliability of Scripture seems to survive in many academic circles despite the repeated collapse of critical theories. One still finds a disposition to trust secular writers whose credentials in providing historical testimony are often less adequate than those of the biblical writers. Not long ago many scholars rejected the historicity of the patriarchal accounts, denied that writing existed in Moses' day, and ascribed the Gospels and Epistles to second-century writers. But higher criticism has sustained some spectacular and even stunning reverses, mainly through the findings of archaeology. No longer is it held that the glories of King Solomon's era are literary fabrication, that 'Yahweh,' the redemptive God of the Hebrews, was unknown before the eighth-century prophets, or that Ezra's representations about the Babylonian captivity are fictional. Archaeologists have located the long-lost copper mines of Solomon's time. Tablets discovered at Ebla near Aleppo confirm that names similar to those of the patriarchs were common among people who lived in Ebla shortly before the events recorded in the later chapters of Genesis took place."

Carl F. H. Henry, "The Authority of the Bible," in *The Origin of the Bible*,
Philip Wesley Comfort, ed., (Wheaton, IL: Tyndale House, 1992) p. 17.

SUMMIT MINISTRIES

FACT

SHEET

**Summit Ministries
does not necessarily endorse all the views and
ideas represented by these sources.**

PO BOX 207
MANITOU SPRINGS, CO 80829
(719) 685-9103

Key Verses

Psalm 14:1; 199:89
Isaiah 40:8
Matthew 5:18; 24:35
Mark 13:31
Luke 1:1-4; 16:17; 21:33
Acts 1:1-3; 2:32

1 Corinthians 15:1-9
2 Timothy 3:16
Hebrews 11:6
2 Peter 1:16
1 John 1:1-3
Revelation 22:18-19

Key Sources

Archer, Gleason L. *Survey of Old Testament Introduction*. Rev. ed. Chicago, IL: Moody, 1994.

Blomberg, Craig. *The Reliability of the Gospels*. Downers Grove, IL: Inter Varsity Press, 1987.

Bruce, F. F. *Are the New Testament Documents Reliable?* 5th ed. Downers Grove, IL: Inter Varsity Press, 1960.

_____. *The Canon of Scripture*. Downers Grove, IL: Inter Varsity Press, 1988.

Carson, D. A., and John D. Woodbridge, eds. *Scripture and Truth*. Grand Rapids, MI: Zondervan, 1983.

_____. *Hermeneutics, Authority and Canon*. Grand Rapids, MI: Zondervan, 1986.

Comfort, Philip Wesley, ed. *The Origin of the Bible*. Wheaton, IL: Tyndale House Publishers, 1992.

Free, Joseph P. *Archaeology and Bible History*. Rev. ed. Grand Rapids, MI: Zondervan, 1992.

Geisler, Norman L., ed. *Inerrancy*. Grand Rapids, MI: Zondervan, 1980.

Geisler, Norman L., and William E. Nix. *A General Introduction to the Bible*. Rev. ed. Chicago, IL: Moody Press, 1968, 1986.

McDowell, Josh. *Evidence That Demands A Verdict*. 2 vols. San Bernardino, CA: Here's Life, (1972) 1979, (1975) 1981.

Thompson, J. A. *The Bible and Archaeology*. Grand Rapids, MI: Eerdmans, 1989.

Warfield, Benjamin B. *The Inspiration and Authority of the Bible*. Phillipsburg, NJ: Presbyterian and Reformed Publishing, 1948. (This is *the* classic on the inspiration, authority and inerrancy of the Bible.)

Key Players

Gleason L. Archer, *Trinity Evangelical Divinity School, Deerfield, IL*
Craig Blomberg, *Denver Seminary, Denver, CO*
F. F. Bruce, (deceased)
D. A. Carson, *Trinity Evangelical Divinity School, Deerfield, IL*
Norman L. Geisler, *Southern Evangelical Seminary, Charlotte, NC*
Walter C. Kaiser, Jr., *Trinity Evangelical Divinity School, Deerfield, IL*
J. I. Packer, *Regent College, B. C., Canada*
Moises Silva, *Westminster Seminary, Philadelphia, PA*
Benjamin B. Warfield, (deceased)

Moral Relativism
UNDERSTANDING THE TIMES

Key Quotes

"There is one thing a professor can be absolutely certain of: almost every student entering the university believes, or says he believes, that truth is relative. If this belief is put to the test, one can count on the students' reaction: They will be uncomprehending. That anyone would regard the proposition as not self-evident astonishes them, as though he were calling into question 2 + 2 = 4.... Openness—and the relativism that makes it the only plausible stance in the face of various claims to truth and various ways of life and kinds of human beings—is the great insight of our times.... The study of history and of culture [according to this view] teaches that all the world was mad in the past; men always thought they were right, and that led to wars, persecutions, slavery, xenophobia, racism, and chauvinism. The point is not to correct the mistakes and really be right; rather it is not to think you are right at all.

"The students, of course, cannot defend their opinion. It is something with which they have been indoctrinated."

Allan Bloom, *The Closing of the American Mind*, (New York: Simon and Schuster, 1987) pp. 25-26.

"The fundamental question of ethics is, who makes the rules? God or men? The theistic answer is that God makes them. The humanist answer is that men make them. This distinction between theism and humanism is the fundamental division in moral theory."

Max Hocutt, "Toward an Ethic of Mutual Accommodation," in *Humanist Ethics*, ed. Morris B. Storer (Buffalo: Prometheus Books, 1980), p. 137.

"No inherent moral or ethical laws exist, nor are there absolute guiding principles for human society. The universe cares nothing for us and we have no ultimate meaning in life."

William Provine, "Scientists, Face It! Science and Religion are Incompatible," *The Scientist*, 5 September 1988, 10.

" . . . we can rationally discuss and argue with each other about right and wrong without resorting to the claim that ethical judgments are merely subjective or relative and that all such judgments have equal validity. For to claim the latter logically leads one to the bizarre judgment that Mother Teresa is no more and no less virtuous than Adolf Hitler."

Frank Beckwith, "Philosophical Problems With Moral Relativism," *Christian Research Journal*, Fall 1993, 39.

"If there is no absolute beyond man's ideas, then there is no final appeal to judge between individuals and groups whose moral judgments conflict. We are merely left with conflicting opinions."

Francis A. Schaeffer, *How Should We Then Live?* (Old Tappan, NJ: Fleming H. Revell, 1976), p. 145.

Key Verses

Exodus 20
Psalm 12:8
Proverbs 14:12; 16:25
Isaiah 5 :20-23
Amos 5:15
Matthew 7:13
Romans 1:18-32; 12:9
Hebrews 5:14

SUMMIT MINISTRIES

FACT SHEET

Summit Ministries does not necessarily endorse all the views and ideas represented by these sources.

PO BOX 207
MANITOU SPRINGS, CO 80829
(719) 685-9103

Key Sources

Bennett, William J., ed. *The Book of Virtues: A Treasury of Great Moral Stories.* New York: Simon and Schuster, 1993.

Beckwith, Francis J., and Michael E. Bauman, eds. *Are You Politically Correct?: Debating America's Cultural Standards.* Buffalo, NY: Prometheus Books, 1993.

Bloom, Alan. *The Closing of the American Mind.* New York: Simon and Schuster, 1987.

Burke, Thomas J., ed. *The Christian Vision: Man and Morality.* Hillsdale, MI: The Hillsdale College Press, 1986.

Davis, John Jefferson. *Evangelical Ethics: Issues Facing the Church Today.* 2nd ed. Phillipsburg, NJ: Presbyterian and Reformed Publishing, 1985, 1993.

Hunter, James Davison. *Culture Wars: The Struggle to Define America.* New York: Basic Books, 1991.

Kilpatrick, William. *Why Johnny Can't Tell Right from Wrong: Moral Illiteracy and the Case for Character Education.* New York: Simon and Schuster, 1992.

Sowell, Thomas. *Inside American Education: The Decline, the Deception, the Dogmas.* New York: The Free Press, 1993.

Sykes, Charles J. *A Nation of Victims: The Decay of the American Character.* New York: St. Martin's Press, 1992.

Key Advocates of Relativism

Joseph Fletcher, *Situation Ethics*, deceased
Paul Kurtz, President, American Humanist Association
Lester Kirkendall, *A New Bill of Sexual Rights and Responsibilities*
Corliss Lamont, *The Philosophy of Humanism*

Feminism
UNDERSTANDING THE TIMES

Key Quotes

"The Christian worldview is intimately familiar with the experience of emptiness, with the despair and impotence that radical feminists – like all of us – seek to escape. We call this experience the human condition. Christians know the dark night of the soul, but we also know that self-glorifying rage will only plunge us deeper into the abyss." Katherine Kersten, "How the Feminist Establishment Hurts Women," *Christianity Today*, June 20, 1994, 25.

"...the only thing so ubiquitous in the feminist's field of vision that she finds it everywhere she looks is herself." Michael Levin, *Feminism and Freedom*, (New Brunswick, NJ: Transaction Books, 1988), p. 300.

"There can't be a relationship where two people are working to make changes in the world. Something has to give. Someone has to be focused on the kids. I think Arnold has made some changes in his life, but one of us had to be flexible enough to be there for our kids all the time." (Maria Shriver articulating what many women have found about "trying to do it all.")
Marilyn Beck, "Maria Shriver Changes Priorities," *Colorado Springs Gazette Telegraph TV Guide*, July 10-16, 1994, 4.

"Feminists are becoming difficult to identify, not because they do not exist, but because their philosophy has been integrated into mainstream society so thoroughly. The philosophy is almost unidentifiable as *feminist*, for it is virtually indistinguishable from *mainstream*."
Mary A. Kassian, *The Feminist Gospel*, (Westchester, IL: Crossway Books, 1922), p. 251.

"I have taught feminist theory. I have debated gender feminists on college campuses around the country, and on national television and radio. My experience with academic feminism and my immersion in the ever-growing gender feminist literature have served to deepen my conviction that the majority of women's studies classes and other classes that teach a 'reconceptualized' subject matter are unscholarly, intolerant of dissent, and full of gimmicks. In other words, they are a waste of time."
Christina Hoff Sommers, *Who Stole Feminism?: How Women Have Betrayed Women*, (New York: Simon & Schuster, 1994), p. 90.

Key Sources

*Blotnick, Srully. *Otherwise Engaged: The Private Lives of Successful Career Women*. New York: Facts on File Publications, 1985. (Reports results of a 25 year study of the professional and private lives of over 2,000 women.)
Kassian, Mary. *The Feminist Gospel*. Westchester, IL: Crossway Books, 1992.
*Farrell, Warren. *The Myth of Male Power*. Simon & Schuster, New York, 1993.
Gilder, George. *Men and Marriage*. Gretna, LA: Pelican, 1986.
*Levin, Michael. *Feminism and Freedom*. New Brunswick, NJ: Transaction Books, 1988.
Mitchell, Brian. *Weak Link: The Feminization of the American Military*. Washington, DC: Regnery-Gateway, 1989.
*Sommers, Cristina Hoff. *Who Stole Feminism? How Women Have Betrayed Women*. New York: Simon & Schuster, 1994.
Piper, John, and Wayne Grudem, eds. *Recovering Biblical Manhood and Womanhood*. Wheaton, IL: Crossway Books, 1991.
See also: "Key Sources" on *Marriage and Family* Fact Sheet.

*These books are not written from a Christian perspective, (and may contain false premises) but will provide some good sources for refuting the ideas of feminism.

Key Verses

Ephesians 2:3, 1 Corinthians 11:10,11, Galatians 3:28, 1 Peter 3:4, Proverbs 31:30

SUMMIT MINISTRIES

FACT
SHEET

Summit Ministries
does not necessarily endorse all the views and
ideas represented by these sources.

PO BOX 207
MANITOU SPRINGS, CO 80829
(719) 685-9103

America's Godly Heritage

UNDERSTANDING THE TIMES

Key Quotes

"... Having undertaken for the Glory of God, and the Advancement of the Christian Faith, and the Honour of our King and Country, a Voyage to plant the first colony in the northern Parts of Virginia; Do by these Presents, solemnly and mutually in the Presence of God and one another, covenant and combine ourselves together into a civil Body Politick...."

The Mayflower Compact, Nov. 11, 1620, reprinted in *Documents of American History*, ed. Henry Steele Commager, 9th ed. (Englewood Cliffs, NJ: Prentice-Hall, 1973), pp. 15-16.

"The general principles, on which the Fathers achieved independence, were ... the general principles of Christianity."

John Adams, in a letter to Thomas Jefferson, June 28, 1813, reprinted in *The Adams-Jefferson Letters*, ed. Lester J. Cappon (Chapel Hill, NC: University of North Carolina Press, 1959), vol. 2, pp. 339-40.

"There is no country in the whole world, in which the Christian religion retains greater influence over the souls of men than in America: and there can be no greater proof of its utility, and of its conformity to human nature, than that its influence is most powerfully felt over the most enlightened and free nation of the earth. [1835]"

Alexis de Tocqueville, *Democracy in America* (New Rochelle, NY: Arlington House, n.d.), vol. 1, p. 294.

"Of all the dispositions and habits which lead to political prosperity, Religion and morality are indispensable supports. In vain would that man claim the tribute of Patriotism, who should labour to subvert these great Pillars of human happiness, these firmest props of the duties of Men and citizens.... And let us with caution indulge the supposition, that morality can be maintained without religion. Whatever may be conceded to the influence of refined education on minds of peculiar structure, reason and experience both forbid us to expect that National morality can prevail in exclusion of religious principle.

"'Tis substantially true, that virtue or morality is a necessary spring of popular government. The rule indeed extends with more or less force to every species of free Government. Who that is sincere friend to it, can look with indifference upon attempts to shake the foundation of the fabric."

George Washington, "Farewell Address," September 19, 1796, in *George Washington: A Collection*, Compiled and Edited by W. B. Allen, (Indianapolis, IN: Liberty *Classics*, 1988), pp. 521-22.

Key Verses

Genesis 9:6
Deuteronomy 8:11-19
2 Chronicles 7:13-14
Judges 2:10-12; 17:6
Job 12:23
Psalms 2; 9:17; 33:12
Proverbs 8:15; 14:34; 29:2
Isaiah 9:6,7
Daniel 2:21; 4:31-32
Romans 13:1-7; 16:25-27
1 Peter 2:13-17

SUMMIT MINISTRIES

FACT SHEET

Summit Ministries does not necessarily endorse all the views and ideas represented by these sources.

PO BOX 207
MANITOU SPRINGS, CO 80829
(719) 685-9103

Being a Christian at the dawn of the twenty-first century can be tough!
You'll need all the help you can get. Help is at hand at the

summit student leadership conference

Join us for a summer conference that will change your life!   Your SUMMIT experience will be unforgettable.
You'll make great friends, ask all the questions you've been dying to ask, and learn how to be successful in life.
This will be the most intense, enjoyable and challenging two weeks you have ever experienced.

what you will learn

THE SUMMIT is far more than a "summer camp" that provides only short-term motivation. At THE SUMMIT you will discover that a worldview based on God's Word is superior to other worldviews.   You will learn how to defend your faith and live life with meaning and purpose from outstanding professors and well-known speakers from around the country.   Topics include

      * Christian apologetics
      * Courtship and marriage
      * The Christian vs. Humanistic, New Age and Marxist worldviews
      * Creation vs. Evolution
      * America's Christian Heritage
      * Free Market vs. Socialism
      * A Biblical response to abortion and homosexuality
      * Leadership and communication skills

In addition, your SUMMIT experience includes developing close friendships during "small group" time, participating in sports activities, going whitewater rafting and hiking, plus delicious meals.

> "I consider Summit Ministries to be one of the very best resources available, and I don't say that lightly!"
> Dr. James Dobson, Focus on the Family

two locations!

THE SUMMIT is currently being held in two locations.   The original SUMMIT at the foot of Pikes Peak in Colorado and SUMMIT EAST held on the campus of Bryan College in Dayton, Tennessee.   Both locations offer the option of earning two or three semester hours of college credit and the same quality teaching.   Recreation and optional activities vary at each location. Call to find out about new locations as they are added.

call today!

Call today for a brochure at the location of your choice.
Sessions fill quickly, so call SUMMIT MINISTRIES at 1-719-685-9103 (Monday -Friday, 9:00 a.m.-5:00 p.m. MST),
or THE SUMMIT AT BRYAN COLLEGE at 1-423-775-7599 (Monday - Friday, 8:30 a.m.-5:00 p.m. EST).

> "Summit Ministries is wonderful. It conveys to students how to think well as Christians. It gives them a model of how to think critically and clearly about their faith. Summit teaches them how to apply the Scriptures to their lives and be prepared for the issues they are going to face at the university."
> Dr. Francis Beckwith, Trinity International University